WILLIAM WORDSWORTH
SAMUEL T. COLERIDGE

Selected Critical Essays

Crofts Classics

GENERAL EDITORS

Samuel H. Beer, *Harvard University*

O. B. Hardison, Jr., *The Folger Shakespeare Library*

John Simon

WILLIAM WORDSWORTH
AND
SAMUEL T. COLERIDGE

Selected
Critical Essays

EDITED BY

Thomas M. Raysor

UNIVERSITY OF NEBRASKA

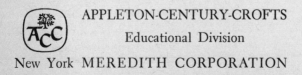

APPLETON-CENTURY-CROFTS

Educational Division

New York MEREDITH CORPORATION

CONTENTS

INTRODUCTION

WHEN WORDSWORTH wrote his Preface to the second edition of *Lyrical Ballads* in 1800, he was reluctant to write "a systematic defence of the theory upon which the poems were based," because the poems should speak for themselves immediately, without argument, or at least without a "systematic" argument extended beyond the limits of a short preface. Nevertheless, the innovations of his style required an explanation to the reader, and the Preface has become famous as the manifesto of the romantic movement in English poetry. With the eloquent additions made in 1802, it deserves its high reputation, though it aroused the private protests of Coleridge in letters to Sotheby and Southey, which he was later to amplify in *Biographia Literaria,* and the public protests of the reviewers, soon to be headed and dominated by Francis Jeffrey, editor of the *Edinburgh Review.* Coleridge's *Biographia Literaria* is both a development of his dissent from Wordsworth's theories of poetry and a defence of the poems, which he thought were exposed unnecessarily to Jeffrey's attacks by the theoretical errors in the Preface. Perhaps, then, the *Biographia Literaria,* however belated, is the true manifesto of romantic poetry.

The Preface dealt chiefly with the style of lyric poetry—condemning a "poetic diction" found only in poetry in favor of a diction common to poetry and prose (in *Lyrical Ballads,* especially the prose of rustic speech), and justifying metrical forms for a diction identical with that of prose. Since lyric poetry cannot depend upon the development of character in action, like drama, this emphasis upon the language and metre of poetry was inevitable. But Wordsworth was too great a poet, not merely in *Lyrical Ballads,* but in other unpublished poetry which he had already composed in 1802, to treat the forms of poetry in such a manner that technique would seem to be an end in itself rather than a means to an end. Though somewhat unsystematically, he states, or implies, a general poetic theory as the basis for his theories of poetic diction. He explains his narrative poetry of rustic life in naturalistic terms as an imitation or representation of reality which is outside the poet, though he enters into it by sharing dramatically the emotions of his characters. Much more explicitly and emphatically, he defines poetry in general in terms of the poet who writes it, as self-expression, as "the spontaneous overflow of powerful feelings." And he defends his poetry, more briefly, in still a third language of poetic theory, not a theory of the reality imitated or represented in poetry, nor a theory of the poet who expresses his intuition of that reality, or expresses his own emotions, but a theory of the effect of poetry upon the reader. Each of his poems "has a worthy *purpose*," he says. Even when without a distinct, conscious purpose, he trusts that in any good poetry the poet's habits of mind will produce poems in which "the understanding of the reader must necessarily be in some degree enlightened and his affections strengthened and purified." Later in the Preface, he adds the remark that the poet "writes under one restriction only, the necessity of giving immediate pleasure." The effect of poetry on the reader is so treated that Wordsworth could easily have accepted the doctrine of Aristotle's *Poetics* (which he seems not to have read): "to learn gives the liveliest pleasure." Or he might be regarded as combining Horace's alternative functions of poetry, "to profit or delight" the reader.

The naturalistic poetry of rustic life, in rustic speech like *The Idiot Boy*, or in the poet's narrative, in dramatic harmony with that speech, like *Michael*, is partly based on Wordsworth's intense social sympathy with humble life, which he merely suggests in his Preface, without detailed argument. He does, however, express his deep faith that in humble rustic life "the passions of men are incorporated with the beautiful and permanent forms of nature," a faith which appears everywhere in Wordsworth's poetry. To Coleridge this seemed to be an illusion. He does not question the influence of nature upon the imagination of a poet, but he argues in *Biographia Literaria* that a prerequisite sensibility and culture, which rustics do not have, is necessary "for the human soul to prosper" in rural life. He is still more convincing in his argument against Wordsworth's proposal to adopt the language of rustics for poetry, even for pastoral poetry. Rustic speech is limited in vocabulary, necessarily factual, disorderly in structure, deficient in the self-consciousness of the poet's mind. "The best part of language," he thought, "is derived from reflection on the acts of the mind itself." Rustics have little part in "these processes and results of imagination." He is arguing against a naturalistic theory of poetry which seems to limit the poet narrowly to the actual life and speech of rustics, and when he analyzes and illustrates the defects of Wordsworth's poetry, he complains justly, like Wordsworth's readers, of an intrusive "matter-of-factness" in a few of the lyrical ballads, and still more, in *The Excursion*. The fault is a consequence of the theories of the Preface, and also, Coleridge feared, of an aspect of Wordsworth's temperament, in startling contrast with his high imagination, in which "he stands nearest of all modern writers to Shakespeare and Milton."

Wordsworth himself says almost nothing in this particular preface about the poet's imagination. His central theme is rather the passion of the poet himself, or the passion of his rustic characters, which he expresses for them. It may sometimes be limited in intensity by Wordsworth's literal and factual naturalism, but, however incongruously, it is his justification for his preference for the life and speech of rustics in poetry: in rustic life, he thought, "the essential passions of the heart find a better soil in which they can attain their maturity." This is the primitivist's belief in uncultivated human nature, which Coleridge did not share. But his disagreement with Wordsworth on the value of rustic life was trivial in comparison with his deeper disagreement on the general significance of passion in poetry. He does not deny the power of passion, for no poet could do that. Indeed his profound and complicated argument against Wordsworth in the eighteenth chapter of *Biographia Literaria* may be condensed into one sentence: "as the *elements* of metre owe their existence to a state of increased excitement, so the metre itself should be accompanied by the natural language of excitement." That is, the passion which expresses itself musically in metre must also express itself in the language of poetry, which is different from the language of prose.

Not only the passion expressed in the poem but the creative passion of the poet himself, generated by "the very act of poetic composition," requires an imaginative and figurative intensity in the language of poetry which would be inappropriate in prose.

But there is more in poetry than "the spontaneous overflow of powerful feelings," either the immediate expression of emotion or the expression of "emotion recollected in tranquillity." Coleridge devotes thirteen chapters of *Biographia Literaria* to a rambling personal narrative and metaphysical argument which culminates in a definition of the imagination. It is an incomplete and highly condensed adaptation of the account of the imagination in the *Transcendental Idealism* of the German philosopher Schelling, and has been the subject of much scholarly controversy. For the metaphysical background, the student must turn to the Introduction to the Oxford edition of *Biographia Literaria* by John Shawcross. But even here, without reference to the idealistic metaphysical argument, one can say that Coleridge regarded the "primary" imagination as the power of the individual consciousness to perceive the external world, in any and every human experience, while the "secondary" imagination, the imagination of the poet, is a rarer quality of the mind which idealizes and shapes its perception of reality into unity. It is still a perception of truth or reality, but it differs from all ordinary perception of daily life because it is not involuntary but coexists "with the conscious will"; that is, it consciously and intentionally shapes the forms of its perception into what is called art.

In chapter fourteen, Coleridge carries on his argument, without metaphysics, by a distinction between a poem and poetry. A poem is an individual work of art, which is distinguished from "works of science" by its *immediate* object, which is pleasure, not truth. Coleridge makes little use, here or elsewhere, of this somewhat inadequate statement of the effect of a poem upon the reader, which is incompatible with the high pretensions of his theory of the imagination, since it has no implications in the perception of truth. Falsehood may please. Moreover, the effect of a poem in giving pleasure cannot easily be attributed to the conscious *purpose* of the poet, unless he is a mere entertainer. Wordsworth kept this more clearly in mind than Coleridge, like Shelley in his *Defense of Poetry*. But Coleridge develops a second principle in his definition of a poem which is more useful for his purpose: a poem must give "such delight from the whole, as is compatible with a distinct gratification from each component part." It is this essential formal principle of an individual work of art, the harmony of the parts with the whole, which enables Coleridge to condemn Wordsworth's lapses into incongruously prosaic diction in verse. But he still has not reached his definition of the nature of poetry, which requires him to turn from the form of an individual poem to the poet, and then to his theory of the poet's imagination. That theory itself needs more amplification and explanation than Coleridge had given it in chapter thirteen, and is not, therefore, a fully satisfactory clue to the nature of the poet as described in chapter fourteen. Yet none the less it is possible to select essential ideas which Coleridge uses for his criticism of Wordsworth. The imagination is still, as we have seen before, a form of conscious perception, "put in action by the will and understanding," not at all an involuntary, spontaneous expression of passion; it shapes into unity "opposite or discordant qualities" in the poet's mind, in the reader's mind, in the work of art, in the relation of the poet's mind or the relation of the poem to nature.

Though Coleridge's condensed list of opposites defies brief comment as completely as the metaphysics of chapter thirteen, we can see again how characteristic it is of his criticism to oppose Wordsworth's extremes and half-truths. He opposes the extremes of Wordsworth's emotionalism as he opposes the extremes of his naturalism. In both cases, he balances against them a sense of the creative power of the poet's mind which he defines as the imagination. There are many passages in Coleridge's criticism in which he shows that the imagination fuses discordant single or multiple images of sense into unity. There are also passages in which the shaping, unifying power of imagination is no more or little more than what Ruskin condescendingly called the "pathetic fallacy," a fallacy of reading into the external world of men and things the personal, unique passions of the poet himself:

The light that never was, on sea or land,
The consecration, and the poet's dream.

If the imagination perceives the symbols of truth by this light, it is only the truth of the poet's own dream. There are other passages in which the imagination has the power of creating an idealistic metaphysical or even religious unity, like that of Wordsworth's Tintern Abbey poem or Immortality Ode. But in all cases, Coleridge defends Wordsworth's poems against the implications of his theory of poetry. And in all cases he does so by insisting that the poet's mind is neither a passive reproduction of external impressions, nor a channel through which his passions rush uncontrolled. It is an active, creative, formative power which shapes the experience of life into art. Not merely in *Biographia Literaria,* but everywhere, Coleridge insists in the manner of the critical and idealistic philosophy of Germany that the human mind shapes its perceptions according to its own forms of thought. The formative power of the mind requires more of poetry than of prose, and creates a language of poetry which is more highly organized in its particular details as well as the whole, unifying thought with feeling, the general idea with the particular image, art with nature. In controversy with Wordsworth on poetic diction he continually illustrates the formative power of the imagination by figures of speech in Wordsworth's (or Shakespeare's) poetry, which Wordsworth had avoided as much as possible in *Lyrical Ballads* and discredited in his Preface, as unusual in the real language of men. And he continually opposes as antithetical half-truths either naturalistic or expressionistic theories of art, because he wishes to combine them into one through the power of the imagination.

TEXTUAL NOTE

The text of Wordsworth's Preface is his final text, that of 1850. The text of Coleridge's *Biographia Literaria* is that of 1817. Both texts are somewhat modernized in such mechanical details as punctuation, capitals within sentences, etc. Frequent misprints in Coleridge's original text are silently corrected.

PRINCIPAL DATES IN THE LIFE OF WILLIAM WORDSWORTH

1770   Born at Cockermouth, Cumberland, April 7.

1787   Entered St. John's College, Cambridge.

1791   B.A. degree, January. Life in London.

1792   Living in France during early French Revolution.

1793   Published *Evening Walk* and *Descriptive Sketches*.

1795-97   Living at Racedown, Dorset.

1797   Moved in July to Alfoxden, Somerset, to be near Coleridge.

1798   Published *Lyrical Ballads*. Travelled in Germany.

1799   In December settled permanently at Grasmere.

1800   Published enlarged edition of *Lyrical Ballads*.

1802   Married Mary Hutchinson.

1807   Published *Poems in Two Volumes*. Badly reviewed.

1808   From this date began to decline in genius.

1814   Published *The Excursion*.

1815   Published collected *Poems,* and *White Doe of Rylstone*.

1813-42   Distributor of stamps for Westmoreland.

1819   Published *Peter Bell,* and *The Waggoner*.

1842-43   Pension; poet laureate.

1850   Death. Posthumous publication of *The Prelude*.

PRINCIPAL DATES IN THE LIFE OF SAMUEL TAYLOR COLERIDGE

1772 Born at Ottery St. Mary, Devon, 21 October.

1791 Entered Jesus College, Cambridge.

1794 Left Cambridge in December, without a degree.

1795 Writing and lecturing in Bristol. Married Sara Fricker.

1796 Conducted a periodical, *The Watchman.*

1797 Lived at Nether Stowey, Somerset. Wordsworth living near, at Alfoxden.

1798 The two poets published *Lyrical Ballads.* Later both in Germany, but separate.

1799 Both returned to England; Coleridge engaged in political journalism.

1800 Coleridge moved to Keswick, to be near Wordsworth at Grasmere.

1801 In ill health, began addiction to opium.

1804 Secretary to the Governor of Malta.

1806 After travel in Italy, returned to England.

1809-10 Living in Wordsworth's family. Published *The Friend* as a periodical.

1811-13 Lecturing and journalism.

1816 Under medical care of James Gillman for remainder of his life.

1817 Published *Biographia Literaria* and collected poems.

1834 Died July 25.

PREFACE

To The Second Edition Of . . .

LYRICAL BALLADS [1]

THE FIRST VOLUME of these poems has already been submitted to general perusal. It was published as an experiment, which, I hoped, might be of some use to ascertain how far, by fitting to metrical arrangement a selection of the real language of men in a state of vivid sensation,[2] that sort of pleasure and that quantity of pleasure may be imparted, which a poet may rationally endeavor to impart.

I had formed no very inaccurate estimate of the probable effect of those poems: I flattered myself that they who should be pleased with them would read them with more than common pleasure: and, on the other hand, I was well aware, that by those who should dislike them they would be read with more than common dislike. The result has differed from my expectation in this only, that a greater number have been pleased than I ventured to hope I should please.

. . . .

Several of my friends are anxious for the success of these poems, from a belief that, if the views with which they were composed were indeed realized, a class of poetry would be produced, well adapted to interest mankind permanently, and not unimportant in the quality and in the multiplicity of its moral relations: and on this

[1] In succeeding editions, when the collection was much enlarged and diversified, this Preface was transferred to the end of the volumes as having little of a special application to their contents (W.'s introductory note).
[2] a selection . . . sensation the language of conversation in the middle and lower classes of society ("Advertisement" to first edition, 1798)

account they have advised me to prefix a systematic
defence of the theory upon which the poems were written.
But I was unwilling to undertake the task, knowing that
on this occasion the reader would look coldly upon my
arguments, since I might be suspected of having been
principally influenced by the selfish and foolish hope of
reasoning him into an approbation of these particular
poems: and I was still more unwilling to undertake the
task, because adequately to display the opinions, and
fully to enforce the arguments, would require a space
wholly disproportionate to a preface. For, to treat the
subject with the clearness and coherence of which it is
susceptible, it would be necessary to give a full account
of the present state of the public taste in this country,
and to determine how far this taste is healthy or depraved;
which, again, could not be determined without pointing
out in what manner language and the human mind act
and re-act on each other, and without retracing the revolu-
tions, not of literature alone, but likewise of society itself.
I have therefore altogether declined to enter regularly
upon this defence; yet I am sensible that there would be
something like impropriety in abruptly obtruding upon the
public, without a few words of introduction, poems so
materially different from those upon which general ap-
probation is at present bestowed.

It is supposed that by the act of writing in verse an
author makes a formal engagement that he will gratify
certain known habits of association; that he not only thus
apprises the reader that certain classes of ideas and ex-
pressions will be found in his book, but that others will
be carefully excluded. This exponent or symbol held forth
by metrical language must in different eras of literature
have excited very different expectations: for example, in
the age of Catullus, Terence, and Lucretius, and that of
Statius or Claudian; and in our own country, in the age of
Shakespeare and Beaumont and Fletcher, and that of
Donne and Cowley, or Dryden, or Pope. I will not take
upon me to determine the exact import of the promise
which, by the act of writing in verse, an author in the
present day makes to his reader; but it will undoubtedly
appear to many persons that I have not fulfilled the terms
of an engagement thus voluntarily contracted. They who

have been accustomed to the gaudiness and inane phraseology of many modern writers, if they persist in reading this book to its conclusion, will, no doubt, frequently have to struggle with feelings of strangeness and awkwardness: they will look round for poetry, and will be induced to inquire by what species of courtesy these attempts can be permitted to assume that title. I hope, therefore, the reader will not censure me for attempting to state what I have proposed to myself to perform; and also (as far as the limits of a preface will permit) to explain some of the chief reasons which have determined me in the choice of my purpose: that at least he may be spared any unpleasant feeling of disappointment, and that I myself may be protected from one of the most dishonorable accusations which can be brought against an author; namely, that of an indolence which prevents him from endeavoring to ascertain what is his duty, or, when his duty is ascertained, prevents him from performing it.

The principal object, then, proposed in these poems was to choose incidents and situations from common life, and to relate or describe them throughout, as far as was possible, in a selection of language really used by men, and, at the same time, to throw over them a certain coloring of imagination, whereby ordinary things should be presented to the mind in an unusual aspect; and further, and above all, to make these incidents and situations interesting by tracing in them, truly though not ostentatiously, the primary laws of our nature: chiefly, as far as regards the manner in which we associate ideas in a state of excitement. Humble and rustic life was generally chosen, because in that condition the essential passions of the heart find a better soil in which they can attain their maturity, are less under restraint, and speak a plainer and more emphatic language; because in that condition of life our elementary feelings co-exist in a state of greater simplicity, and, consequently, may be more accurately contemplated, and more forcibly communicated; because the manners of rural life germinate from those elementary feelings, and, from the necessary character of rural occupations, are more easily comprehended, and are more durable; and, lastly, because in that condition the passions of men are incorporated with the beautiful and permanent

forms of nature. The language, too, of these men has been
adopted (purified indeed from what appear to be its real
defects, from all lasting and rational causes of dislike or
disgust), because such men hourly communicate with the
best objects from which the best part of language is
originally derived; and because, from their rank in society
and the sameness and narrow circle of their intercourse,
being less under the influence of social vanity, they convey
their feelings and notions in simple and unelaborated ex-
pressions. Accordingly, such a language, arising out of
repeated experience and regular feelings, is a more
permanent, and a far more philosophical language than
that which is frequently substituted for it by poets, who
think that they are conferring honor upon themselves and
their art in proportion as they separate themselves from
the sympathies of men, and indulge in arbitrary and
capricious habits of expression, in order to furnish food
for fickle tastes and fickle appetites of their own creation.[3]

I cannot, however, be insensible to the present outcry
against the triviality and meanness, both of thought and
language, which some of my contemporaries have oc-
casionally introduced into their metrical compositions; and
I acknowledge that this defect, where it exists, is more
dishonorable to the writer's own character than false re-
finement or arbitrary innovation, though I should contend
at the same time that it is far less pernicious in the sum of
its consequences. From such verses the poems in these
volumes will be found distinguished at least by one mark
of difference, that each of them has a worthy *purpose*.
Not that I always began to write with a distinct purpose
formally conceived, but habits of meditation have, I trust,
so prompted and regulated my feelings, that my descrip-
tions of such objects as strongly excite those feelings will
be found to carry along with them a *purpose*. If this
opinion be erroneous, I can have little right to the name
of a poet. For all good poetry is the spontaneous overflow
of powerful feelings: and though this be true, poems to
which any value can be attached were never produced on
any variety of subjects but by a man who, being possessed

[3] It is worth while here to observe, that the affecting parts of
Chaucer are almost always expressed in language pure and
universally intelligible even to this day (W.'s note).

of more than usual organic sensibility, had also thought long and deeply. For our continued influxes of feeling are modified and directed by our thoughts, which are indeed the representatives of all our past feelings; and as, by contemplating the relation of these general representatives to each other, we discover what is really important to men, so, by the repetition and continuance of this act, our feelings will be connected with important subjects, till at length, if we be originally possessed of much sensibility, such habits of mind will be produced that, by obeying blindly and mechanically the impulses of those habits, we shall describe objects, and utter sentiments, of such a nature, and in such connection with each other, that the understanding of the reader must necessarily be in some degree enlightened, and his affections strengthened and purified.

It has been said that each of these poems has a purpose. Another circumstance must be mentioned which distinguishes these poems from the popular poetry of the day; it is this, that the feeling therein developed gives importance to the action and situation, and not the action and situation to the feeling.

A sense of false modesty shall not prevent me from asserting that the reader's attention is pointed to this mark of distinction, far less for the sake of these particular poems than from the general importance of the subject. The subject is indeed important! For the human mind is capable of being excited without the application of gross and violent stimulants; and he must have a very faint perception of its beauty and dignity who does not know this, and who does not further know, that one being is elevated above another in proportion as he possesses this capability. It has therefore appeared to me, that to endeavor to produce or enlarge this capability is one of the best services in which, at any period, a writer can be engaged; but this service, excellent at all times, is especially so at the present day. For a multitude of causes, unknown to former times, are now acting with a combined force to blunt the discriminating powers of the mind, and, unfitting it for all voluntary exertion, to reduce it to a state of almost savage torpor. The most effective of these causes are the great national events

which are daily taking place, and the increasing accu-
mulation of men in cities, where the uniformity of their
occupations produces a craving for extraordinary incident
which the rapid communication of intelligence hourly
gratifies. To this tendency of life and manners the litera-
ture and theatrical exhibitions of the country have con-
formed themselves. The invaluable works of our elder
writers, I had almost said the works of Shakespeare and
Milton, are driven into neglect by frantic novels, sickly
and stupid German tragedies, and deluges of idle and
extravagant stories in verse.—When I think upon this
degrading thirst after outrageous stimulation, I am almost
ashamed to have spoken of the feeble endeavor made in
these volumes to counteract it; and, reflecting upon the
magnitude of the general evil, I should be oppressed with
no dishonorable melancholy, had I not a deep impression
of certain inherent and indestructible qualities of the
human mind, and likewise of certain powers in the great
and permanent objects that act upon it, which are equally
inherent and indestructible; and were there not added to
this impression a belief that the time is approaching when
the evil will be systematically opposed by men of greater
powers, and with far more distinguished success.

Having dwelt thus long on the subjects and aim of these
poems, I shall request the reader's permission to apprise
him of a few circumstances relating to their *style,* in order,
among other reasons, that he may not censure me for not
having performed what I never attempted. The reader will
find that personifications of abstract ideas rarely occur in
these volumes, and are utterly rejected as an ordinary
device to elevate the style and raise it above prose. My
purpose was to imitate, and, as far as is possible, to adopt
the very language of men; and assuredly such personifica-
tions do not make any natural or regular part of that
language. They are, indeed, a figure of speech occasionally
prompted by passion, and I have made use of them as
such; but have endeavored utterly to reject them as a
mechanical device of style, or as a family language which
writers in metre seem to lay claim to by prescription. I
have wished to keep the reader in the company of flesh
and blood, persuaded that by so doing I shall interest him.
Others who pursue a different track will interest him

likewise; I do not interfere with their claim, but wish to prefer a claim of my own. There will also be found in these volumes little of what is usually called poetic diction; as much pains has been taken to avoid it as is ordinarily taken to produce it; this has been done for the reason already alleged, to bring my language near to the language of men; and further, because the pleasure which I have proposed to myself to impart is of a kind very different from that which is supposed by many persons to be the proper object of poetry. Without being culpably particular, I do not know how to give my reader a more exact notion of the style in which it was my wish and intention to write, than by informing him that I have at all times endeavored to look steadily at my subject; consequently there is, I hope, in these poems little falsehood of description, and my ideas are expressed in language fitted to their respective importance. Something must have been gained by this practice, as it is friendly to one property of all good poetry, namely, good sense: but it has necessarily cut me off from a large portion of phrases and figures of speech which from father to son have long been regarded as the common inheritance of poets. I have also thought it expedient to restrict myself still further, having abstained from the use of many expressions, in themselves proper and beautiful, but which have been foolishly repeated by bad poets, till such feelings of disgust are connected with them as it is scarcely possible by any art of association to overpower.

If in a poem there should be found a series of lines, or even a single line, in which the language, though naturally arranged, and according to the strict laws of metre, does not differ from that of prose, there is a numerous class of critics who, when they stumble upon these prosaisms, as they call them, imagine that they have made a notable discovery, and exult over the poet as over a man ignorant of his own profession. Now these men would establish a canon of criticism which the reader will conclude he must utterly reject, if he wishes to be pleased with these volumes. And it would be a most easy task to prove to him that not only the language of a large portion of every good poem, even of the most elevated character, must necessarily, except with reference to the metre, in no respect

differ from that of good prose, but likewise that some of
the most interesting parts of the best poems will be found
to be strictly the language of prose when prose is well
written. The truth of this assertion might be demonstrated
by innumerable passages from almost all the poetical
writings, even of Milton himself. To illustrate the subject
in a general manner, I will here adduce a short com-
position of Gray, who was at the head of those who, by
their reasonings, have attempted to widen the space of
separation betwixt prose and metrical composition, and
was more than any other man curiously elaborate in the
structure of his own poetic diction.

> In vain to me the smiling mornings shine,
> And reddening Phoebus lifts his golden fire:
> The birds in vain their amorous descant join,
> Or cheerful fields resume their green attire.
> These ears, alas! for other notes repine;
> *A different object do these eyes require;*
> *My lonely anguish melts no heart but mine;*
> *And in my breast the imperfect joys expire;*
> Yet morning smiles the busy race to cheer,
> And new-born pleasure brings to happier men;
> The fields to all their wonted tribute bear;
> To warm their little loves the birds complain.
> *I fruitless mourn to him that cannot hear,*
> *And weep the more because I weep in vain.*[4]

It will easily be perceived, that the only part of this
sonnet which is of any value is the lines printed in italics;
it is equally obvious that, except in the rhyme and in the
use of the single word "fruitless" for fruitlessly, which is
so far a defect, the language of these lines does in no
respect differ from that of prose.

By the foregoing quotation it has been shown that the
language of prose may yet be well adapted to poetry; and
it was previously asserted that a large portion of the
language of every good poem can in no respect differ
from that of good prose. We will go further. It may be
safely affirmed that there neither is, nor can be, any
essential difference between the language of prose and
metrical composition. We are fond of tracing the resem-

---

[4] vain "Sonnet on the Death of Richard West"

blance between poetry and painting, and, accordingly, we call them sisters: but where shall we find bonds of connection sufficiently strict to typify the affinity betwixt metrical and prose composition? They both speak by and to the same organs; the bodies in which both of them are clothed may be said to be of the same substance, their affections are kindred, and almost identical, not necessarily differing even in degree; poetry[5] sheds no tears "such as angels weep," [6] but natural and human tears; she can boast of no celestial ichor that distinguishes her vital juices from those of prose; the same human blood circulates through the veins of them both.

If it be affirmed that rhyme and metrical arrangement of themselves constitute a distinction which overturns what has just been said on the strict affinity of metrical language with that of prose, and paves the way for other artificial distinctions which the mind voluntarily admits, I answer that the[7] language of such poetry as is here

[5] I here use the word "poetry" (though against my own judgment) as opposed to the word "prose," and synonymous with metrical composition. But much confusion has been introduced into criticism by this contradistinction of poetry and prose, instead of the more philosophical one of poetry and matter of fact, or science. The only strict antithesis to prose is metre; nor is this, in truth, a *strict* antithesis, because lines and passages of metre so naturally occur in writing prose, that it would be scarcely possible to avoid them, even were it desirable (W.'s note, based probably on an article by William Enfield in the *Monthly Magazine,* July, 1796. Enfield opposes poetry to philosophy. See Aristotle's distinction of poetry and history, *Poetics,* ch. IX. These theoretical distinctions are all far too important for a footnote. See Abrams, *The Mirror and the Lamp,* ch. XI.)
[6] weep Milton's *Paradise Lost,* I, 619
[7] the first word of a long addition to the Preface made in 1802. The 1800 text resumes on p. 17. See n. 11. Including the Appendix, the text of 1802 is approximately twice as long as the Preface of 1800; and the additions indicate an important change of emphasis in Wordsworth's poetic theory. His naturalistic emphasis in defending poetry of rustic life in rustic speech now changes to an expressionist emphasis on the poet himself. W. argues that he expresses his own passions even in dramatic poems, since he has identified himself with the passions of his characters. This argument still limits the poet's own creative

recommended is, as far as is possible, a selection of the
language really spoken by men; that this selection, wher-
ever it is made with true taste and feeling, will of itself
form a distinction far greater than would at first be
imagined, and will entirely separate the composition from
the vulgarity and meanness of ordinary life; and, if metre
be superadded thereto, I believe that a dissimilitude will
be produced altogether sufficient for the gratification of a
rational mind. What other distinction would we have?
Whence is it to come? And where is it to exist? Not,
surely, where the poet speaks through the mouths of his
characters: it cannot be necessary here, either for eleva-
tion of style, or any of its supposed ornaments; for, if the
poet's subject be judiciously chosen, it will naturally, and
upon fit occasion, lead him to passions the language of
which, if selected truly and judiciously, must necessarily
be dignified and variegated, and alive with metaphors and
figures. I forbear to speak of an incongruity which would
shock the intelligent reader, should the poet interweave
any foreign splendor of his own with that which the pas-
sion naturally suggests: it is sufficient to say that such
addition is unnecessary. And, surely, it is more probable
that those passages which with propriety abound with
metaphors and figures, will have their due effect if, upon
other occasions where the passions are of a milder char-
acter, the style also be subdued and temperate.

But, as the pleasure which I hope to give by the poems
now presented to the reader must depend entirely on just
notions upon this subject, and as it is in itself of high im-
portance to our taste and moral feelings, I cannot content
myself with these detached remarks. And if, in what I am
about to say, it shall appear to some that my labor is
unnecessary, and that I am like a man fighting a battle
without enemies, such persons may be reminded that,
whatever be the language outwardly holden by men, a
practical faith in the opinions which I am wishing to
establish is almost unknown. If my conclusions are

---

contribution to his poems, and forces W. to slip into several
naturalistic admissions of the superiority of nature to the
dramatic art of narrative poetry. But at least he makes clearer
his conception of poetry as the expression of passion.

admitted, and carried as far as they must be carried if admitted at all, our judgments concerning the works of the greatest poets, both ancient and modern, will be far different from what they are at present, both when we praise and when we censure: and our moral feelings influencing and influenced by these judgments will, I believe, be corrected and purified.

Taking up the subject, then, upon general grounds, let me ask, what is meant by the word poet? What is a poet? To whom does he address himself? And what language is to be expected from him?—He is a man speaking to men: a man, it is true, endowed with more lively sensibility, more enthusiasm and tenderness, who has a greater knowledge of human nature, and a more comprehensive soul, than are supposed to be common among mankind; a man pleased with his own passions and volitions, and who rejoices more than other men in the spirit of life that is in him; delighting to contemplate similar volitions and passions as manifested in the goings-on of the universe, and habitually impelled to create them where he does not find them. To these qualities he has added a disposition to be affected more than other men by absent things as if they were present; an ability of conjuring up in himself passions, which are indeed far from being the same as those produced by real events, yet (especially in those parts of the general sympathy which are pleasing and delightful) do more nearly resemble the passions produced by real events than anything which, from the motions of their own minds merely, other men are accustomed to feel in themselves:—whence, and from practice, he has acquired a greater readiness and power in expressing what he thinks and feels, and especially those thoughts and feelings which, by his own choice, or from the structure of his own mind, arise in him without immediate external excitement.

But whatever portion of this faculty we may suppose even the greatest poet to possess, there cannot be a doubt that the language which it will suggest to him must often, in liveliness and truth, fall short of that which is uttered by men in real life under the actual pressure of those passions, certain shadows of which the poet thus produces, or feels to be produced, in himself.

However exalted a notion we would wish to cherish of the character of a poet, it is obvious that, while he describes and imitates passions, his employment is in some degree mechanical, compared with the freedom and power of real and substantial action and suffering. So that it will be the wish of the poet to bring his feelings near to those of the persons whose feelings he describes, nay, for short spaces of time, perhaps, to let himself slip into an entire delusion, and even confound and identify his own feelings with theirs; modifying only the language which is thus suggested to him by a consideration that he describes for a particular purpose, that of giving pleasure. Here, then, he will apply the principle of selection which has been already insisted upon. He will depend upon this for removing what would otherwise be painful or disgusting in the passion; he will feel that there is no necessity to trick out or to elevate nature: and the more industriously he applies this principle, the deeper will be his faith that no words which *his* fancy or imagination can suggest, will be to be compared with those which are the emanations of reality and truth.

But it may be said by those who do not object to the general spirit of these remarks, that, as it is impossible for the poet to produce upon all occasions language as exquisitely fitted for the passion as that which the real passion itself suggests, it is proper that he should consider himself as in the situation of a translator, who does not scruple to substitute excellences of another kind for those which are unattainable by him; and endeavors occasionally to surpass his original, in order to make some amends for the general inferiority to which he feels that he must submit. But this would be to encourage idleness and unmanly despair. Further, it is the language of men who speak of what they do not understand; who talk of poetry as of a matter of amusement and idle pleasure; who will converse with us as gravely about a *taste* for poetry, as they express it, as if it were a thing as indifferent as a taste for rope-dancing, or Frontiniac or Sherry. Aristotle, I have been told, has said, that poetry is the most philosophic[8] of all writing: it is so: its object is

---

[8] **philosophic** more philosophic than history (*Poetics*, IX)

truth, not individual and local, but general and operative; not standing upon external testimony, but carried alive into the heart by passion; truth which is its own testimony, which gives competence and confidence to the tribunal to which it appeals, and receives them from the same tribunal. Poetry is the image of man and nature. The obstacles which stand in the way of the fidelity of the biographer and historian, and of their consequent utility, are incalculably greater than those which are to be encountered by the poet who comprehends the dignity of his art. The poet writes under one restriction only, namely, the necessity of giving immediate pleasure to a human being possessed of that information which may be expected from him, not as a lawyer, a physician, a mariner, an astronomer, or a natural philosopher, but as a man. Except this one restriction, there is no object standing between the poet and the image of things; between this, and the biographer and historian, there are a thousand.

Nor let this necessity of producing immediate pleasure be considered as a degradation of the poet's art. It is far otherwise. It is an acknowledgment of the beauty of the universe,[9] an acknowledgment the more sincere, because not formal, but indirect; it is a task light and easy to him who looks at the world in the spirit of love: further, it is a homage paid to the native and naked dignity of man, to the grand elementary principle of pleasure, by which he knows, and feels, and lives, and moves. We have no sympathy but what is propagated by pleasure: I would not be misunderstood; but wherever we sympathise with pain, it will be found that the sympathy is produced and carried on by subtle combinations with pleasure. We have no knowledge, that is, no general principles drawn from the contemplation of particular facts, but what has been built up by pleasure, and exists in us by pleasure alone.

[9] **universe** this pleasure of poetry is, therefore, the pleasure of the poet himself. Compare the noble treatments of this theme in Wordsworth's poetry, especially in *The Prelude*. In writing his poem, the poet may have no conscious purpose like that of the didactic poet or the mere entertainer, but his *effect* upon the reader will be to give "immediate pleasure," because the reader will share the pleasure of the poet sympathetically, and his "affections" will be "strengthened and purified."

The man of science, the chemist and mathematician, whatever difficulties and disgusts they may have had to struggle with, know and feel this. However painful may be the objects with which the anatomist's knowledge is connected, he feels that his knowledge is pleasure; and where he has no pleasure he has no knowledge. What then does the poet? He considers man and the objects that surround him as acting and re-acting upon each other, so as to produce an infinite complexity of pain and pleasure; he considers man in his own nature and in his ordinary life as contemplating this with a certain quantity of immediate knowledge, with certain convictions, intuitions, and deductions, which from habit acquire the quality of intuitions; he considers him as looking upon this complex scene of ideas and sensations, and finding everywhere objects that immediately excite in him sympathies which, from the necessities of his nature, are accompanied by an overbalance of enjoyment.

To this knowledge which all men carry about with them, and to these sympathies in which, without any other discipline than that of our daily life, we are fitted to take delight, the poet principally directs his attention. He considers man and nature as essentially adapted to each other, and the mind of man as naturally the mirror of the fairest and most interesting properties of nature. And thus the poet, prompted by this feeling of pleasure, which accompanies him through the whole course of his studies, converses with general nature, with affections akin to those which, through labor and length of time, the man of science has raised up in himself, by conversing with those particular parts of nature which are the objects of his studies. The knowledge both of the poet and the man of science is pleasure; but the knowledge of the one cleaves to us as a necessary part of our existence, our natural and unalienable inheritance; the other is a personal and individual acquisition, slow to come to us, and by no habitual and direct sympathy connecting us with our fellow-beings. The man of science seeks truth as a remote and unknown benefactor; he cherishes and loves it in his solitude: the poet, singing a song in which all human beings join with him, rejoices in the presence of truth as our visible friend and hourly companion. Poetry is the breath and finer spirit of all knowledge; it is the impassioned expression which is in the countenance of all science. Emphatically may it be said of the poet, as Shakespeare[10] hath said of man, "that he looks before and after." He is the rock of defence for human nature; an upholder and preserver, carrying everywhere with him relationship and love. In spite of difference of soil and climate, of language and manners, of laws and customs: in spite of things silently gone out of mind, and things violently destroyed, the poet binds together by passion and knowledge the vast empire of human society, as it is spread over the whole earth and over all time. The objects of the poet's thoughts are everywhere; though the eyes and senses of man are, it is true, his favorite guides, yet he will follow wheresoever he can find an atmosphere of sensation in which to move his wings. Poetry is the first and last of all knowledge—it is as immortal as the heart of man. If the labors of men of science should ever create any material revolution, direct or indirect, in our condition, and in the impressions which we habitually receive, the poet will sleep then no more than at present; he will be ready to follow the steps of the man of science, not only in those general indirect effects, but he will be at his side, carrying sensation into the midst of the objects of the science itself. The remotest discoveries of the chemist, the botanist, or mineralogist, will be as proper objects of the poet's art as any upon which it can be employed, if the time should ever come when these things shall be familiar to us, and the relations under which they are contemplated by the followers of these respective sciences shall be manifestly and palpably material to us as enjoying and suffering beings. If the time should ever come when what is now called science, thus familiarised to men, shall be ready to put on, as it were, a form of flesh and blood, the poet will lend his divine spirit to aid the transfiguration, and will welcome the being thus produced as a dear and genuine inmate of the household of man.—It is not, then, to be supposed that any one who holds that sublime notion of poetry which I have attempted to convey, will break in upon the sanctity and

[10] **Shakespeare** cf. *Hamlet*, IV, iv, 37

truth of his pictures by transitory and accidental orna-
ments, and endeavor to excite admiration of himself by
arts, the necessity of which must manifestly depend upon
the assumed meanness of his subject.

What has been thus far said applies to poetry in gen-
eral, but especially to those parts of composition where the
poet speaks through the mouths of his characters; and
upon this point it appears to authorise the conclusion that
there are few persons of good sense who would not allow
that the dramatic parts of composition are defective, in
proportion as they deviate from the real language of
nature, and are colored by a diction of the poet's own,
either peculiar to him as an individual poet or belonging
simply to poets in general; to a body of men who, from
the circumstance of their compositions being in metre, it
is expected will employ a particular language.

It is not, then, in the dramatic parts of composition that
we look for this distinction of language; but still it may
be proper and necessary where the poet speaks to us in
his own person and character. To this I answer by re-
ferring the reader to the description before given of a
poet. Among the qualities there enumerated as principally
conducing to form a poet, is implied nothing differing in
kind from other men, but only in degree. The sum of what
was said is, that the poet is chiefly distinguished from
other men by a greater promptness to think and feel
without immediate external excitement, and a greater
power in expressing such thoughts and feelings as are
produced in him in that manner. But these passions and
thoughts and feelings are the general passions and
thoughts and feelings of men. And with what are they
connected? Undoubtedly with our moral sentiments and
animal sensations, and with the causes which excite these;
with the operations of the elements, and the appearances
of the visible universe; with storm and sunshine, with the
revolutions of the seasons, with cold and heat, with loss
of friends and kindred, with injuries and resentments,
gratitude and hope, with fear and sorrow. These, and the
like, are the sensations and objects which the poet de-
scribes, as they are the sensations of other men, and the
objects which interest them. The poet thinks and feels
in the spirit of human passions. How, then, can his lan-

guage differ in any material degree from that of all other men who feel vividly and see clearly? It might be *proved* that it is impossible. But supposing that this were not the case, the poet might then be allowed to use a peculiar language when expressing his feelings for his own gratification, or that of men like himself. But poets do not write for poets alone, but for men. Unless, therefore, we are advocates for that admiration which subsists upon ignorance, and that pleasure which arises from hearing what we do not understand, the poet must descend from this supposed height; and, in order to excite rational sympathy, he must express himself as other men express themselves. To this it may be added, that while he is only selecting from the real language of men, or, which amounts to the same thing, composing accurately in the spirit of such selection, he is treading upon safe ground, and we know what we are to expect from him. Our feelings are the same with respect to metre; for, as it may be proper to remind the reader,[11] the distinction of metre is regular and uniform, and not, like that which is produced by what is usually called POETIC DICTION, arbitrary, and subject to infinite caprices, upon which no calculation whatever can be made. In the one case, the reader is utterly at the mercy of the poet, respecting what imagery or diction he may choose to connect with the passion; whereas, in the other, the metre obeys certain laws, to which the poet and reader both willingly submit because they are certain, and because no interference is made by them with the passion but such as the concurring testimony of ages has shown to heighten and improve the pleasure which co-exists with it.

It will now be proper to answer an obvious question, namely, Why, professing these opinions, have I written in verse? To this, in addition to such answer as is included in what has been already said, I reply, in the first place, because, however I may have restricted myself, there is still left open to me what confessedly constitutes the most valuable object of all writing, whether in prose or verse; the great and universal passions of men, the most general and interesting of their occupations, and the entire

[11] **reader** last word of the long passage added in 1802

world of nature before me—to supply endless combinations of forms and imagery. Now, supposing for a moment that whatever is interesting in these objects may be as vividly described in prose, why should I be condemned for attempting to superadd to such description the charm which, by the consent of all nations, is acknowledged to exist in metrical language? To this, by such as are yet unconvinced, it may be answered that a very small part of the pleasure given by poetry depends upon the metre, and that it is injudicious to write in metre, unless it be accompanied with the other artificial distinctions of style with which metre is usually accompanied, and that, by such deviation, more will be lost from the shock which will thereby be given to the reader's associations than will be counterbalanced by any pleasure which he can derive from the general power of numbers. In answer to those who still contend for the necessity of accompanying metre with certain appropriate colors of style in order to the accomplishment of its appropriate end, and who also, in my opinion, greatly underrate the power of metre in itself, it might, perhaps, as far as relates to these volumes, have been almost sufficient to observe, that poems are extant, written upon more humble subjects, and in a still more naked and simple style, which have continued to give pleasure from generation to generation. Now, if nakedness and simplicity be a defect, the fact here mentioned affords a strong presumption that poems somewhat less naked and simple are capable of affording pleasure at the present day; and what I wished *chiefly* to attempt, at present, was to justify myself for having written under the impression of this belief.

But various causes might be pointed out why, when the style is manly, and the subject of some importance, words metrically arranged will long continue to impart such a pleasure to mankind as he who proves the extent of that pleasure will be desirous to impart. The end of poetry is to produce excitement in co-existence with an overbalance of pleasure; but, by the supposition, excitement is an unusual and irregular state of the mind; ideas and feelings do not, in that state, succeed each other in accustomed order. If the words, however, by which this excitement is produced be in themselves powerful, or the images and feelings have an undue proportion of pain connected with them, there is some danger that the excitement may be carried beyond its proper bounds. Now the co-presence of something regular, something to which the mind has been accustomed in various moods and in a less excited state, cannot but have great efficacy in tempering and restraining the passion by an intertexture of ordinary feeling, and of feeling not strictly and necessarily connected with the passion. This is unquestionably true; and hence, though the opinion will at first appear paradoxical, from the tendency of metre to divest language, in a certain degree, of its reality, and thus to throw a sort of half-consciousness of unsubstantial existence over the whole composition, there can be little doubt but that more pathetic situations and sentiments, that is, those which have a greater proportion of pain connected with them, may be endured in metrical composition, especially in rhyme, than in prose. The metre of the old ballads is very artless; yet they contain many passages which would illustrate this opinion; and, I hope, if the following poems be attentively perused, similar instances will be found in them. This opinion may be further illustrated by appealing to the reader's own experience of the reluctance with which he comes to the re-perusal of the distressful parts of "Clarissa Harlowe," or the "Gamester";[12] while Shakespeare's writings, in the most pathetic scenes, never act upon us as pathetic beyond the bounds of pleasure—an effect which, in a much greater degree than might at first be imagined, is to be ascribed to small, but continual and regular impulses of pleasurable surprise from the metrical arrangement.—On the other hand (what it must be allowed will much more frequently happen), if the poet's words should be incommensurate with the passion, and inadequate to raise the reader to a height of desirable excitement, then (unless the poet's choice of his metre has been grossly injudicious) in the feelings of pleasure which the reader has been accustomed to connect with metre in general, and in the feeling, whether cheerful or melancholy, which he has been accustomed to

[12] Gamester a domestic tragedy by Edward Moore, pub. 1753

connect with that particular movement of metre, there will be found something which will greatly contribute to impart passion to the words, and to effect the complex end which the poet proposes to himself.

If I had undertaken a SYSTEMATIC defence of the theory here maintained, it would have been my duty to develop the various causes upon which the pleasure received from metrical language depends. Among the chief of these causes is to be reckoned a principle which must be well known to those who have made any of the arts the object of accurate reflection; namely, the pleasure which the mind derives from the perception of similitude in dissimilitude. This principle is the great spring of the activity of our minds, and their chief feeder. From this principle the direction of the sexual appetite, and all the passions connected with it, take their origin; it is the life of our ordinary conversation; and upon the accuracy with which similitude in dissimilitude, and dissimilitude in similitude, are perceived, depend our taste and our moral feelings. It would not be a useless employment to apply this principle to the consideration of metre, and to show that metre is hence enabled to afford much pleasure, and to point out in what manner that pleasure is produced. But my limits will not permit me to enter upon this subject, and I must content myself with a general summary.

I have said that poetry is the spontaneous overflow of powerful feelings: it takes its origin from emotion recollected in tranquillity; the emotion is contemplated till, by a species of re-action, the tranquillity gradually disappears, and an emotion, kindred to that which was before the subject of contemplation, is gradually produced, and does itself actually exist in the mind. In this mood successful composition generally begins, and in a mood similar to this it is carried on; but the emotion, of whatever kind, and in whatever degree, from various causes, is qualified by various pleasures, so that in describing any passions whatsoever, which are voluntarily described, the mind will, upon the whole, be in a state of enjoyment. If nature be thus cautious to preserve in a state of enjoyment a being so employed, the poet ought to profit by the lesson held forth to him, and ought especially to take care that, whatever passions he communicates to his reader, those passions, if his reader's mind be sound and vigorous, should always be accompanied with an overbalance of pleasure. Now the music of harmonious metrical language, the sense of difficulty overcome, and the blind association of pleasure which has been previously received from works of rhyme or metre of the same or similar construction, an indistinct perception perpetually renewed of language closely resembling that of real life, and yet, in the circumstance of metre, differing from it so widely—all these imperceptibly make up a complex feeling of delight, which is of the most important use in tempering the painful feeling always found intermingled with powerful descriptions of the deeper passions. This effect is always produced in pathetic and impassioned poetry; while in lighter compositions, the ease and gracefulness with which the poet manages his numbers are themselves confessedly a principal source of the gratification of the reader. All that it is *necessary* to say, however, upon this subject, may be effected by affirming, what few persons will deny, that of two descriptions, either of passions, manners, or characters, each of them equally well executed, the one in prose and the other in verse, the verse will be read a hundred times where the prose is read once.

Having thus explained a few of my reasons for writing in verse, and why I have chosen subjects from common life, and endeavored to bring my language near to the real language of men, if I have been too minute in pleading my own cause, I have at the same time been treating a subject of general interest; and for this reason a few words shall be added with reference solely to these particular poems, and to some defects which will probably be found in them. I am sensible that my associations must have sometimes been particular instead of general, and that, consequently, giving to things a false importance, I may have sometimes written upon unworthy subjects; but I am less apprehensive on this account, than that my language may frequently have suffered from those arbitrary connections of feelings and ideas with particular words and phrases from which no man can altogether protect himself. Hence I have no doubt that, in some instances, feelings, even of the ludicrous, may be given to my readers by expressions which appeared to me tender and pathetic. Such

faulty expressions, were I convinced they were faulty at
present, and that they must necessarily continue to be
so, I would willingly take all reasonable pains to correct.
But it is dangerous to make these alterations on the simple
authority of a few individuals, or even of certain classes
of men; for where the understanding of an author is not
convinced, or his feelings altered, this cannot be done
without great injury to himself: for his own feelings are
his stay and support; and, if he set them aside in one
instance, he may be induced to repeat this act till his mind
shall lose all confidence in itself, and become utterly debili-
tated. To this it may be added, that the critic ought never
to forget that he is himself exposed to the same errors as
the poet, and, perhaps, in a much greater degree: for
there can be no presumption in saying of most readers,
that it is not probable they will be so well acquainted with
the various stages of meaning through which words have
passed, or with the fickleness or stability of the relations
of particular ideas to each other; and, above all, since they
are so much less interested in the subject, they may
decide lightly and carelessly.

Long as the reader has been detained, I hope he will
permit me to caution him against a mode of false criticism
which has been applied to poetry in which the language
closely resembles that of life and nature. Such verses
have been triumphed over in parodies, of which Dr. John-
son's stanza is a fair specimen:—

> I put my hat upon my head
> And walked into the Strand,
> And there I met another man
> Whose hat was in his hand.[18]

Immediately under these lines let us place one of the
most justly-admired stanzas of the "Babes in the Wood."

> These pretty babes with hand in hand
> Went wandering up and down;
> But never more they saw the man
> Approaching from the town.

[18] **hand** *Poems* (Oxford, 1941), pp. 156-58. A parody of a ballad
by Bishop Percy.

In both these stanzas the words, and the order of the
words, in no respect differ from the most unimpassioned
conversation. There are words in both, for example, "the
Strand," and "the town," connected with none but the
most familiar ideas; yet the one stanza we admit as ad-
mirable, and the other as a fair example of the superla-
tively contemptible. Whence arises this difference? Not
from the metre, not from the language, not from the order
of the words; but the *matter* expressed in Dr. Johnson's
stanza is contemptible. The proper method of treating
trivial and simple verses, to which Dr. Johnson's stanza
would be a fair parallelism, is not to say, this is a bad
kind of poetry, or, this is not poetry; but, this wants sense;
it is neither interesting in itself, nor can *lead* to anything
interesting; the images neither originate in that same state
of feeling which arises out of thought, nor can excite
thought or feeling in the reader. This is the only sensible
manner of dealing with such verses. Why trouble yourself
about the species till you have previously decided upon the
genus? Why take pains to prove that an ape is not a New-
ton, when it is self-evident that he is not a man? [14]

One request I must make of my reader, which is, that
in judging these poems he would decide by his own feel-
ings genuinely, and not by reflection upon what will prob-
ably be the judgment of others. How common is it to hear
a person say, I myself do not object to this style of com-
position, or this or that expression, but to such and such
classes of people it will appear mean or ludicrous! This
mode of criticism, so destructive of all sound unadulterated
judgment, is almost universal: let the reader then abide,
independently, by his own feelings, and, if he finds him-
self affected, let him not suffer such conjectures to inter-
fere with his pleasure.

If an author, by any single composition, has impressed
us with respect for his talents, it is useful to consider this
as affording a presumption that on other occasions where
we have been displeased he, nevertheless, may not have
written ill or absurdly; and further, to give him so much
credit for this one composition as may induce us to review
what has displeased us with more care than we should

[14] **man** a reference to Pope's *Essay on Man,* II, 34

otherwise have bestowed upon it. This is not only an act of justice, but, in our decisions upon poetry especially, may conduce, in a high degree, to the improvement of our own taste; for an *accurate* taste in poetry, and in all the other arts, as Sir Joshua Reynolds[15] has observed, is an *acquired* talent, which can only be produced by thought and a long-continued intercourse with the best models of composition. This is mentioned, not with so ridiculous a purpose as to prevent the most inexperienced reader from judging for himself (I have already said that I wish him to judge for himself), but merely to temper the rashness of decision, and to suggest that, if poetry be a subject on which much time has not been bestowed, the judgment may be erroneous; and that, in many cases, it necessarily will be so.

Nothing would, I know, have so effectually contributed to further the end which I have in view, as to have shown of what kind the pleasure is, and how that pleasure is produced, which is confessedly produced by metrical composition essentially different from that which I have here endeavored to recommend: for the reader will say that he has been pleased by such composition; and what more can be done for him? The power of any art is limited; and he will suspect that, if it be proposed to furnish him with new friends, that can be only upon condition of his abandoning his old friends. Besides, as I have said, the reader is himself conscious of the pleasure which he has received from such composition, composition to which he has peculiarly attached the endearing name of poetry; and all men feel an habitual gratitude, and something of an honorable bigotry, for the objects which have long continued to please them: we not only wish to be pleased, but to be pleased in that particular way in which we have been accustomed to be pleased. There is in these feelings enough to resist a host of arguments; and I should be the less able to combat them successfully, as I am willing to allow that, in order entirely to enjoy the poetry which I am recommending, it would be necessary to give up much of what is ordinarily enjoyed. But would my limits have permitted me to point out how this pleasure is produced, many obstacles might have been removed, and the reader

[15] Reynolds *Discourses*, II, VI, VIII

assisted in perceiving that the powers of language are not
so limited as he may suppose; and that it is possible for
poetry to give other enjoyments, of a purer, more lasting,
and more exquisite nature. This part of the subject has
not been altogether neglected, but it has not been so much
my present aim to prove that the interest excited by some
other kinds of poetry is less vivid, and less worthy of the
nobler powers of the mind, as to offer reasons for presum-
ing that if my purpose were fulfilled, a species of poetry
would be produced which is genuine poetry; in its nature
well adapted to interest mankind permanently, and like-
wise important in the multiplicity and quality of its moral
relations.

From what has been said, and from a perusal of the
poems, the reader will be able clearly to perceive the
object which I had in view: he will determine how far
it has been attained; and, what is a much more important
question, whether it be worth attaining: and upon the
decision of these two questions will rest my claim to the
approbation of the public.

APPENDIX[1]

Perhaps, as I have no right to expect that attentive
perusal, without which, confined, as I have been, to the
narrow limits of a preface, my meaning cannot be thor-
oughly understood, I am anxious to give an exact notion
of the sense in which the phrase poetic diction has been
used; and for this purpose, a few words shall here be
added, concerning the origin and characteristics of the
phraseology which I have condemned under that name.

The earliest poets of all nations generally wrote from
passion excited by real events; they wrote naturally, and
as men: feeling powerfully as they did, their language was

---

[1] **Appendix** See p. 17, by what is usually called POETIC
DICTION. (W.'s introductory note. This is the second great
addition in 1802 to the Preface, and is included here, because
W. makes clear his conception of "poetic diction." Since it is
obviously possible for a modern poet, like W., to use the
figurative language of "passion," if he has passion, like the
earliest poets, this argument was easy for C. to answer in ch.
XVIII).

daring, and figurative. In succeeding times, poets, and men ambitious of the fame of poets, perceiving the influence of such language, and desirous of producing the same effect without being animated by the same passion, set themselves to a mechanical adoption of these figures of speech, and made use of them, sometimes with propriety, but much more frequently applied them to feelings and thoughts with which they had no natural connection whatsoever. A language was thus insensibly produced, differing materially from the real language of men in *any situation*. The reader or hearer of this distorted language found himself in a perturbed and unusual state of mind: when affected by the genuine language of passion he had been in a perturbed and unusual state of mind also: in both cases he was willing that his common judgment and understanding should be laid asleep, and he had no instinctive and infallible perception of the true to make him reject the false; the one served as a passport for the other. The emotion was in both cases delightful, and no wonder if he confounded the one with the other, and believed them both to be produced by the same or similar causes. Besides, the poet spake to him in the character of a man to be looked up to, a man of genius and authority. Thus, and from a variety of other causes, this distorted language was received with admiration; and poets, it is probable, who had before contented themselves for the most part with misapplying only expressions which at first had been dictated by real passion, carried the abuse still further, and introduced phrases composed apparently in the spirit of the original figurative language of passion, yet altogether of their own invention, and characterised by various degrees of wanton deviation from good sense and nature.

It is indeed true that the language of the earliest poets was felt to differ materially from ordinary language, because it was the language of extraordinary occasions; but it was really spoken by men, language which the poet himself had uttered when he had been affected by the events which he described, or which he had heard uttered by those around him. To this language it is probable that metre of some sort or other was early superadded. This separated the genuine language of poetry still further from common life, so that whoever read or heard the poems of these earliest poets felt himself moved in a way in which he had not been accustomed to be moved in real life, and by causes manifestly different from those which acted upon him in real life. This was the great temptation to all the corruptions which have followed: under the protection of this feeling succeeding poets constructed a phraseology which had one thing, it is true, in common with the genuine language of poetry, namely, that it was not heard in ordinary conversation; that it was unusual. But the first poets, as I have said, spake a language which, though unusual, was still the language of men. This circumstance, however, was disregarded by their successors; they found that they could please by easier means: they became proud of modes of expression which they themselves had invented, and which were uttered only by themselves. In process of time metre became a symbol or promise of this unusual language, and whoever took upon him to write in metre, according as he possessed more or less of true poetic genius, introduced less or more of this adulterated phraseology into his compositions, and the true and the false were inseparably interwoven until, the taste of men becoming gradually perverted, this language was received as a natural language, and at length, by the influence of books upon men, did to a certain degree really become so. Abuses of this kind were imported from one nation to another, and with the progress of refinement this diction became daily more and more corrupt, thrusting out of sight the plain humanities of nature by a motley masquerade of tricks, quaintnesses, hieroglyphics, and enigmas.[2]

[2] **enigmas** the remaining half of the Appendix consists chiefly of illustrations of poetic diction in Dr. Johnson and Cowper

BIOGRAPHIA LITERARIA

CHAPTER XIV

Occasion of the Lyrical Ballads, and the objects originally proposed—Preface to the second edition—The ensuing controversy, its causes and acrimony—Philosophic definitions of a poem and poetry with scholia.

DURING THE first year that Mr. Wordsworth and I were neighbors, our conversations turned frequently on the two cardinal points of poetry, the power of exciting the sympathy of the reader by a faithful adherence to the truth of nature, and the power of giving the interest of novelty by the modifying colors of imagination. The sudden charm which accidents of light and shade, which moon-light or sun-set diffused over a known and familiar landscape, appeared to represent the practicability of combining both. These are the poetry of nature. The thought suggested itself (to which of us I do not recollect) that a series of poems might be composed of two sorts. In the one, the incidents and agents were to be, in part at least, supernatural; and the excellence aimed at was to consist in the interesting of the affections by the dramatic truth of such emotions as would naturally accompany such situations, supposing them real. And real in *this* sense they have been to every human being who, from whatever source of delusion, has at any time believed himself under supernatural agency. For the second class, subjects were to be chosen from ordinary life; the characters and incidents were to be such as will be found in every village and its vicinity, where there is a meditative and feeling mind to seek after them, or to notice them, when they present themselves.

In this idea originated the plan of the "Lyrical Ballads"; in which it was agreed, that my endeavors should be directed to persons and characters supernatural, or at least

romantic; yet so as to transfer from our inward nature a
human interest and a semblance of truth sufficient to pro-
cure for these shadows of imagination that willing suspen-
sion of disbelief for the moment, which constitutes poetic
faith.[1] Mr. Wordsworth, on the other hand, was to propose
to himself as his object, to give the charm of novelty to
things of every day, and to excite a feeling analogous to
the supernatural, by awakening the mind's attention from
the lethargy of custom, and directing it to the loveliness
and the wonders of the world before us; an inexhaustible
treasure, but for which, in consequence of the film of fa-
miliarity and selfish solicitude we have eyes, yet see not,
ears that hear not, and hearts that neither feel nor under-
stand.

With this view I wrote "The Ancient Mariner," and
was preparing among other poems, "The Dark Ladie," and
the "Christabel," in which I should have more nearly
realized my ideal than I had done in my first attempt. But
Mr. Wordsworth's industry had proved so much more suc-
cessful, and the number of his poems so much greater,
that my compositions, instead of forming a balance, ap-
peared rather an interpolation of heterogeneous matter.
Mr. Wordsworth added two or three poems written in his
own character, in the impassioned, lofty, and sustained
diction which is characteristic of his genius. In this form
the "Lyrical Ballads" were published; and were presented
by him, as an *experiment,* whether subjects, which from
their nature rejected the usual ornaments and extra-
colloquial style of poems in general, might not be so
managed in the language of ordinary life as to produce
the pleasurable interest which it is the peculiar business of
poetry to impart. To the second edition he added a preface
of considerable length; in which, notwithstanding some
passages of apparently a contrary import, he was under-
stood to contend for the extension of this style to poetry
of all kinds, and to reject as vicious and indefensible all

[1] **poetic faith** a memorable definition which is here modestly
phrased with reference to C.'s own "supernatural, or at least
romantic" poetry, but is developed elsewhere to distinguish
poetic (or dramatic) reality from mere fact. See p. 91, below;
Biog. Lit. (Shawcross), II, 187; *Shakespearean Criticism*
(Raysor), I, 127-131, 199-202.

phrases and forms of style that were not included in what he (unfortunately, I think, adopting an equivocal expression) called the language of *real* life. From this preface, prefixed to poems in which it was impossible to deny the presence of original genius, however mistaken its direction might be deemed, arose the whole long-continued controversy. For from the conjunction of perceived power with supposed heresy I explain the inveteracy and in some instances, I grieve to say, the acrimonious passions, with which the controversy has been conducted by the assailants.

Had Mr. Wordsworth's poems been the silly, the childish things, which they were for a long time described as being; had they been really distinguished from the compositions of other poets merely by meanness of language and inanity of thought; had they indeed contained nothing more than what is found in the parodies and pretended imitations of them; they must have sunk at once, a dead weight, into the slough of oblivion, and have dragged the preface along with them. But year after year increased the number of Mr. Wordsworth's admirers. They were found too not in the lower classes of the reading public, but chiefly among young men of strong sensibility and meditative minds; and their admiration (inflamed perhaps in some degree by opposition) was distinguished by its intensity, I might almost say, by its *religious* fervor. These facts, and the intellectual energy of the author, which was more or less consciously felt, where it was outwardly and even boisterously denied, meeting with sentiments of aversion to his opinions, and of alarm at their consequences, produced an eddy of criticism, which would of itself have borne up the poems by the violence with which it whirled them round and round. With many parts of this preface, in the sense attributed to them, and which the words undoubtedly seem to authorize, I never concurred; but on the contrary objected [2] to them as erroneous in principle, and as contradictory (in appearance at least) both to other parts of the same preface, and to the

[2] objected *Letters:* To Sotheby, 13 July, 1802; To Southey, 29 July, 1802. But, W.'s "preface is half a child of my own brain" (To Southey).

author's own practice in the greater number of the poems
themselves. Mr. Wordsworth in his recent collection has,
I find, degraded this prefatory disquisition to the end of
his second volume, to be read or not at the reader's choice.
But he has not, as far as I can discover, announced any
change in his poetic creed. At all events, considering it
as the source of a controversy, in which I have been hon-
ored more than I deserve by the frequent conjunction
of my name with his, I think it expedient to declare once
for all, in what points I coincide with his opinions, and
in what points I altogether differ. But in order to render
myself intelligible I must previously, in as few words as
possible, explain my ideas, first, of a POEM; and secondly,
of POETRY itself, in *kind,* and in *essence.*[3]

The office of philosophical *disquisition* consists in just
distinction; while it is the privilege of the philosopher to
preserve himself constantly aware, that distinction is not
division. In order to obtain adequate notions of any truth,
we must intellectually separate its distinguishable parts;
and this is the technical *process* of philosophy. But having
so done, we must then restore them in our conceptions to
the unity in which they actually co-exist; and this is the
result of philosophy. A poem contains the same elements
as a prose composition; the difference therefore must con-
sist in a different combination of them, in consequence
of a different object proposed. According to the difference
of the object will be the difference of the combination. It
is possible that the object may be merely to facilitate the
recollection of any given facts or observations by artificial
arrangement; and the composition will be a poem, merely
because it is distinguished from prose by metre, or by
rhyme, or by both conjointly. In this, the lowest sense, a
man might attribute the name of a poem to the well-known
enumeration of the days in the several months:

[3] **essence** the second section of R. S. Crane's essay listed in the
Bibliography explains the importance in poetics of this distinc-
tion of the poem and poetry, the individual work of art and
the imagination which produces it.—From this point to the end
of the chapter, C. is rewriting his own lectures of 1808 and
1811-12. Cf. *Shakespearean Criticism,* I, 163-167; II, 64-99.

Thirty days hath September,
April, June, and November, &c.

and others of the same class and purpose. And as a particular pleasure is found in anticipating the recurrence of sounds and quantities, all compositions that have this charm superadded, whatever be their contents, *may* be entitled poems.

So much for the superficial *form*. A difference of object and contents supplies an additional ground of distinction. The immediate purpose may be the communication of truths; either of truth absolute and demonstrable, as in works of science; or of facts experienced and recorded, as in history. Pleasure, and that of the highest and most permanent kind, may *result* from the *attainment* of the end; but it is not itself the immediate end. In other works the communication of pleasure may be the immediate purpose; and though truth, either moral or intellectual, ought to be the *ultimate* end, yet this will distinguish the character of the author, not the class to which the work belongs. Blest indeed is that state of society in which the immediate purpose would be baffled by the perversion of the proper ultimate end; in which no charm of diction or imagery could exempt the Bathyllus even of an Anacreon,[4] or the Alexis of Virgil,[5] from disgust and aversion!

But the communication of pleasure may be the immediate object of a work not metrically composed; and that object may have been in a high degree attained, as in novels and romances. Would then the mere superaddition of metre, with or without rhyme, entitle *these* to the name of poems? The answer is, that nothing can permanently please which does not contain in itself the reason why it is so, and not otherwise. If metre be superadded, all other parts must be made consonant with it. They must be such as to justify the perpetual and distinct attention to each part which an exact correspondent recurrence of accent and sound are calculated to excite. The final definition then, so deduced, may be thus worded. A poem is that species of composition, which is opposed to works of science, by proposing for its *immediate* object pleasure,

[4] **Anacreon** seventeenth ode (no longer attributed to Anacreon)
[5] **Virgil** second eclogue

could it be main = TRUE OR whatever possible

not truth; and from all other species (having *this* object in common with it) it is discriminated by proposing to itself such delight from the *whole,* as is compatible with a distinct gratification from each component *part.*[6]

Controversy is not seldom excited in consequence of the disputants attaching each a different meaning to the same word; and in few instances has this been more striking than in disputes concerning the present subject. If a man chooses to call every composition a poem which is rhyme, or measure, or both, I must leave his opinion uncontroverted. The distinction is at least competent to characterize the writer's intention. If it were subjoined that the whole is likewise entertaining or affecting, as a tale, or as a series of interesting reflections, I of course admit this as another fit ingredient of a poem, and an additional merit. But if the definition sought for be that of a *legitimate* poem, I answer, it must be one, the parts of which mutually support and explain each other; all in their proportion harmonizing with, and supporting the purpose and known influences of metrical arrangement. The philosophic critics of all ages coincide with the ultimate judgment of all countries, in equally denying the praises of a just poem, on the one hand, to a series of striking lines or distichs, each of which, absorbing the whole attention of the reader to itself, disjoins it from its context, and makes it a separate whole, instead of an harmonizing part; and on the other hand, to an unsustained composition, from which the reader collects rapidly the general result, unattracted by the component parts. The reader should be carried forward, not merely or chiefly by the mechanical impulse of curiosity, or by a restless desire to arrive at the final solution; but by the pleasurable activity of mind excited by the attractions of the journey itself. Like the motion of a serpent, which the Egyptians made the emblem of intellectual power; or like the path of sound

[6] part the two preceding paragraphs are not in harmony with the aesthetics of either Kant or Schelling, but rather with British hedonism, and a poetics based on rhetoric, since they treat the pleasure of the reader as the *purpose* of the poet. The pleasure of the reader is treated by Wordsworth, more effectively, as the communication of the previous pleasure of the poet; that is, as a result rather than a purpose.

through the air; at every step he pauses and half recedes, and from the retrogressive movement collects the force which again carries him onward. "Praecipitandus est *liber* spiritus," says Petronius[7] Arbiter most happily. The epithet, *liber*, here balances the preceding verb; and it is not easy to conceive more meaning condensed in fewer words.

But if this should be admitted as a satisfactory character of a poem, we have still to seek for a definition of poetry. The writings of PLATO, and Bishop TAYLOR, and the "Theoria Sacra" of BURNET, furnish undeniable proofs that poetry of the highest kind may exist without metre, and even without the contra-distinguishing objects of a poem. The first chapter of Isaiah (indeed a very large proportion of the whole book) is poetry in the most emphatic sense; yet it would be not less irrational than strange to assert that pleasure, and not truth, was the immediate object of the prophet. In short, whatever *specific* import we attach to the word poetry, there will be found involved in it, as a necessary consequence, that a poem of any length neither can be, nor ought to be, all poetry. Yet if an harmonious whole is to be produced, the remaining parts must be preserved *in keeping* with the poetry; and this can be no otherwise effected than by such a studied selection and artificial arrangement, as will partake of *one*, though not a *peculiar* property of poetry. And this again can be no other than the property of exciting a more continuous and equal attention than the language of prose aims at, whether colloquial or written.

My own conclusions on the nature of poetry, in the strictest use of the word, have been in part anticipated in the preceding disquisition on the fancy and imagination. What is poetry? is so nearly the same question with, what is a poet? that the answer to the one is involved in the solution of the other. For it is a distinction resulting from the poetic genius itself, which sustains and modifies the images, thoughts, and emotions of the poet's own mind.

The poet, described in *ideal* perfection, brings the whole soul of man into activity, with the subordination of its

---

[7] Petronius *Satyricon*, 118: "the free spirit must be hurried onward."

faculties to each other, according to their relative worth and dignity. He diffuses a tone and spirit of unity that blends, and (as it were) *fuses*, each into each, by that synthetic and magical power to which we have exclusively appropriated the name of imagination. This power, first put in action by the will and understanding, and retained under their irremissive, though gentle and unnoticed, control (*laxis effertur habenis*)[8] reveals itself in the balance or reconciliation of opposite or discordant qualities: of sameness, with difference; of the general, with the concrete; the idea, with the image; the individual, with the representative; the sense of novelty and freshness, with old and familiar objects; a more than usual state of emotion, with more than usual order; judgment ever awake and steady self-possession, with enthusiasm and feeling profound or vehement; and while it blends and harmonizes the natural and the artificial, still subordinates art to nature; the manner to the matter; and our admiration of the poet to our sympathy with the poetry. "Doubtless," as Sir John Davies[9] observes of the soul (and his words may with slight alteration be applied, and even more appropriately, to the poetic IMAGINATION),

> Doubtless this could not be, but that she turns
> Bodies to spirit by sublimation strange,
> As fire converts to fire the things it burns,
> As we our food into our nature change.
>
> From their gross matter she abstracts their forms,
> And draws a kind of quintessence from things;
> Which to her proper nature she transforms,
> To bear them light on her celestial wings.
>
> Thus does she, when from individual states
> She doth abstract the universal kinds;
> Which then re-clothed in divers names and fates
> Steal access through our senses to our minds.

Finally, good sense is the body of poetic genius, fancy its drapery, motion its life, and imagination the soul that is everywhere, and in each; and forms all into one graceful and intelligent whole.

[8] habenis "is borne on with loose reins." Virgil's *Georgics*, II, 364.
[9] Davies in Section IV of *Nosce Teipsum* (altered)

Chapter XVII

*Examination of the tenets peculiar to Mr. Wordsworth—
Rustic life (above all, low and rustic life) especially un-
favorable to the formation of a human diction—The best
parts of language the product of philosophers, not clowns
or shepherds—Poetry essentially ideal and generic—The
language of Milton as much the language of real life, yea,
incomparably more so than that of the cottager.*

As FAR THEN as Mr. Wordsworth in his preface con-
tended, and most ably contended, for a reformation in
our poetic diction, as far as he has evinced the truth of
passion, and the *dramatic* propriety of those figures and
metaphors in the original poets, which stripped of their
justifying reasons, and converted into mere artifices of
connection or ornament, constitute the characteristic falsity
in the poetic style of the moderns; and as far as he has,
with equal acuteness and clearness, pointed out the
process by which this change was effected, and the resem-
blances between that state into which the reader's mind
is thrown by the pleasurable confusion of thought from
an unaccustomed train of words and images; and that
state which is induced by the natural language of impas-
sioned feeling; he undertook a useful task, and deserves
all praise, both for the attempt and for the execution. The
provocations to this remonstrance in behalf of truth and
nature were still of perpetual recurrence before and after
the publication of this preface. I cannot likewise but add
that the comparison of such poems of merit as have been
given to the public within the last ten or twelve years, with
the majority of those produced previously to the appear-
ance of that preface, leave no doubt on my mind that Mr.
Wordsworth is fully justified in believing his efforts to
have been by no means ineffectual. Not only in the verses
of those who have professed their admiration of his genius,
but even of those who have distinguished themselves by
hostility to his theory, and depreciation of his writings, are
the impressions of his principles plainly visible. It is pos-
sible that with these principles others may have been
blended, which are not equally evident; and some which

are unsteady and subvertible from the narrowness or imperfection of their basis. But it is more than possible that these errors of defect or exaggeration, by kindling and feeding the controversy, may have conduced not only to the wider propagation of the accompanying truths, but that, by their frequent presentation to the mind in an excited state, they may have won for them a more permanent and practical result. A man will borrow a part from his opponent the more easily, if he feels himself justified in continuing to reject a part. While there remain important points in which he can still feel himself in the right, in which he still finds firm footing for continued resistance, he will gradually adopt those opinions which were the least remote from his own convictions, as not less congruous with his own theory than with that which he reprobates. In like manner with a kind of instinctive prudence, he will abandon by little and little his weakest posts, till at length he seems to forget that they had ever belonged to him, or affects to consider them at most as accidental and "petty annexments," the removal of which leaves the citadel unhurt and unendangered.

My own differences from certain supposed parts of Mr. Wordsworth's theory ground themselves on the assumption that his words had been rightly interpreted, as purporting that the proper diction for poetry in general consists altogether in a language taken, with due exceptions, from the mouths of men in real life, a language which actually constitutes the natural conversation of men under the influence of natural feelings. My objection is, first, that in *any* sense this rule is applicable only to *certain* classes of poetry; secondly, that even to these classes it is not applicable, except in such a sense, as hath never by any one (as far as I know or have read) been denied or doubted; and lastly, that as far as, and in that degree in which it is *practicable*, yet as a *rule* it is useless, if not injurious, and therefore either need not, or ought not to be practised. The poet informs his reader that he had generally chosen *low*[1] and *rustic* life; but not *as* low and rustic, or in order to repeat that pleasure of doubtful moral

[1] low 1800-1827 text; *humble* 1832. "Low" is a condescending word in classical criticism, which W. used with defiant praise.

effect which persons of elevated rank and of superior re-
finement oftentimes derive from a happy *imitation* of the
rude unpolished manners and discourse of their inferiors.
For the pleasure so derived may be traced to three exciting
causes. The first is the naturalness, in *fact,* of the things
represented. The second is the apparent naturalness of the
representation, as raised and qualified by an imperceptible
infusion of the author's own knowledge and talent, which
infusion does, indeed, constitute it an *imitation* as dis-
tinguished from a mere *copy.*[2] The third cause may be
found in the reader's conscious feeling of his superiority
awakened by the contrast presented to him; even as for
the same purpose the kings and great barons of yore re-
tained sometimes *actual* clowns and fools, but more fre-
quently shrewd and witty fellows in that *character.* These,
however, were not Mr. Wordsworth's objects. *He* chose
low and rustic life, "because in that condition the essen-
tial passions of the heart find a better soil in which they
can attain their maturity, are less under restraint, and
speak a plainer and more emphatic language; because in
that condition of life our elementary feelings coexist in
a state of greater simplicity, and consequently may be
more accurately contemplated, and more forcibly com-
municated; because the manners of rural life germinate
from those elementary feelings; and from the necessary
character of rural occupations are more easily compre-
hended, and are more durable; and lastly, because in that
condition the passions of men are incorporated with the
beautiful and permanent forms of nature."

Now it is clear to me that in the most interesting of the
poems, in which the author is more or less dramatic, as
"The Brothers," "Michael," "Ruth," "The Mad Mother,"
&c., the persons introduced are by no means taken *from
low or rustic life* in the common acceptation of those
words; and it is not less clear that the sentiments and
language, as far as they can be conceived to have been
really transferred from the minds and conversation of

[2] This is a favorite distinction, which permits C. to attack a
naturalistic, literal copy of human nature either as a subjective
romantic critic, or as an objective classical critic, emphasizing
general human nature. See Index, *Biog. Lit.* (Shawcross);
Shakespearean Criticism (Raysor).

such persons, are attributable to causes and circumstances not necessarily connected with "their occupations and abode." The thoughts, feelings, language, and manners of the shepherd-farmers in the vales of Cumberland and Westmoreland, as far as they are actually adopted in those poems, may be accounted for from causes which will and do produce the same results in *every* state of life, whether in town or country. As the two principal I rank that INDEPENDENCE which raises a man above servitude, or daily toil for the profit of others, yet not above the necessity of industry and a frugal simplicity of domestic life; and the accompanying unambitious, but solid and religious EDUCATION which has rendered few books familiar but the Bible, and the liturgy or hymn book. To this latter cause, indeed, which is so far *accidental* that it is the blessing of particular countries and a particular age, not the product of particular places or employments, the poet owes the show of probability that his personages might really feel, think, and talk with any tolerable resemblance to his representation. It is an excellent remark of Dr. Henry More's (*Enthusiasmus triumphatus*, Sec. XXXV), that "a man of confined education, but of good parts, by constant reading of the Bible will naturally form a more winning and commanding rhetoric than those that are learned; the intermixture of tongues and of artificial phrases debasing *their* style."

It is, moreover, to be considered that to the formation of healthy feelings, and a reflecting mind, *negations* involve impediments not less formidable than sophistication and vicious intermixture. I am convinced that for the human soul to prosper in rustic life a certain vantage-ground is pre-requisite. It is not every man that is likely to be improved by a country life or by country labors. Education, or original sensibility, or both, must pre-exist, if the changes, forms, and incidents of nature are to prove a sufficient stimulant. And where these are not sufficient, the mind contracts and hardens by want of stimulants; and the man becomes selfish, sensual, gross, and hard-hearted. Let the management of the POOR LAWS in Liverpool, Manchester, or Bristol be compared with the ordinary dispensation of the poor rates in agricultural villages, where the *farmers* are the overseers and guardians of the poor. If my own experience have not been particularly unfortunate, as well as that of the many respectable country clergymen with whom I have conversed on the subject, the result would engender more than scepticism concerning the desirable influences of low and rustic life in and for itself. Whatever may be concluded on the other side, from the stronger local attachments and enterprizing spirit of the Swiss, and other mountaineers, applies to a particular mode of pastoral life, under forms of property that permit and beget manners truly republican, not to rustic life in general, or to the absence of artificial cultivation. On the contrary the mountaineers whose manners have been so often eulogized, are in general better educated and greater readers than men of equal rank elsewhere. But where this is not the case, as among the peasantry of North Wales, the ancient mountains, with all their terrors and all their glories, are pictures to the blind, and music to the deaf.

I should not have entered so much into detail upon this passage, but here seems to be the point, to which all the lines of difference converge as to their source and centre. (I mean, as far as, and in whatever respect, my poetic creed *does* differ from the doctrines promulged in this preface.) I adopt with full faith the principle of Aristotle that poetry as poetry is essentially *ideal*,[3] that it avoids and excludes all *accident;* that its apparent individualities of rank, character, or occupation must be *representative* of a class; and that the *persons* of poetry must be clothed with

[4] Say not that I am recommending abstractions, for these class-characteristics which constitute the instructiveness of a character, are so modified and particularized in each person of the Shakespearean drama that life itself does not excite more distinctly that sense of individuality which belongs to real existence. Paradoxical as it may sound, one of the essential properties of geometry is not less essential to dramatic excellence; and Aristotle has accordingly required of the poet an involution of the universal in the individual. The chief differences are that in geometry it is the universal truth which is uppermost in the consciousness; in poetry the individual form in which the truth is clothed. (C.'s note, much shortened. He quotes from his periodical of 1809-10, *The Friend,* the second letter of Satyrane. The reference to Aristotle is to the *Poetics,* IX).

generic attributes, with the *common* attributes of the class; not with such as one gifted individual might *possibly* possess, but such as from his situation it is most probable beforehand that he *would* possess. If my premises are right and my deductions legitimate, it follows that there can be no *poetic* medium between the swains of Theocritus and those of an imaginary golden age.

The characters of the vicar and the shepherd-mariner in the poem of "THE BROTHERS," that of the shepherd of Greenhead Ghyll in the "MICHAEL," have all the verisimilitude and representative quality, that the purposes of poetry can require. They are persons of a known and abiding class, and their manners and sentiments the natural product of circumstances common to the class. Take "MICHAEL" for instance:

> An old man, stout of heart, and strong of limb;
> His bodily frame had been from youth to age
> Of an unusual strength: his mind was keen,
> Intense and frugal, apt for all affairs,
> And in his shepherd's calling he was prompt
> And watchful more than ordinary men.
> Hence he had learned the meaning of all winds,
> Of blasts of every tone; and oftentimes
> When others heeded not, he heard the South
> Make subterraneous music, like the noise
> Of bagpipers on distant Highland hills.
> The shepherd, at such warning, of his flock
> Bethought him, and he to himself would say,
> The winds are now devising work for me!
> And truly at all times the storm, that drives
> The traveller to a shelter, summoned him
> Up to the mountains. He had been alone
> Amid the heart of many thousand mists,
> That came to him and left him on the heights.
> So lived he till his eightieth year was passed
> And grossly that man errs, who should suppose
> That the green valleys, and the streams and rocks,
> Were things indifferent to the shepherd's thoughts.
> Fields, where with cheerful spirits he had breathed
> The common air; the hills, which he so oft
> Had climbed with vigorous steps; which had impressed
> So many incidents upon his mind
> Of hardship, skill or courage, joy or fear;
> Which like a book preserved the memory

Of the dumb animals, whom he had saved,
Had fed or sheltered, linking to such acts,
So grateful in themselves, the certainty
Of honorable gain; these fields, these hills
Which were his living being, even more
Than his own blood—what could they less? had laid
Strong hold on his affections, were to him
A pleasurable feeling of blind love,
The pleasure which there is in life itself.

On the other hand, in the poems which are pitched at a
lower note, as the "HARRY GILL," "IDIOT BOY," &c.,
the *feelings* are those of human nature in general; though
the poet has judiciously laid the *scene* in the country,
in order to place *himself* in the vicinity of interesting
images, without the necessity of ascribing a sentimental
perception of their beauty to the persons of his drama.
In "The Idiot Boy," indeed, the mother's character is not
so much a real and native product of a "situation where
the essential passions of the heart find a better soil in
which they can attain their maturity and speak a plainer
and more emphatic language," as it is an impersonation
of an instinct abandoned by judgment. Hence the two
following charges seem to me not wholly groundless: at
least, they are the only plausible objections which I have
heard to that fine poem. The one is that the author has
not, in the poem itself, taken sufficient care to preclude
from the reader's fancy the disgusting images of *ordinary,
morbid idiocy*, which yet it was by no means his intention
to represent. He has even by the "burr, burr, burr," un-
counteracted by any preceding description of the boy's
beauty, assisted in recalling them. The other is that the
idiocy of the *boy* is so evenly balanced by the folly of the
mother, as to present to the general reader rather a laugh-
able burlesque on the blindness of anile dotage, than an
analytic display of maternal affection in its ordinary work-
ings.

In "The Thorn" the poet himself acknowledges in a
note the necessity of an introductory poem, in which he
should have portrayed the character of the person from
whom the words of the poem are supposed to proceed: a
superstitious man moderately imaginative, of slow facul-
ties and deep feelings, "a captain of a small trading vessel,

for example, who, being past the middle age of life, had retired upon an annuity, or small independent income, to some village or country town of which he was not a native, or in which he had not been accustomed to live. Such men having nothing to do become credulous and talkative from indolence." But in a poem, still more in a lyric poem (and the NURSE in Shakespeare's *Romeo and Juliet* alone prevents me from extending the remark even to dramatic *poetry,* if indeed the Nurse itself can be deemed altogether a case in point), it is not possible to imitate truly a dull and garrulous discourser, without repeating the effects of dullness and garrulity. However this may be, I dare assert that the parts (and these form the far larger portion of the whole) which might as well or still better have proceeded from the poet's own imagination, and have been spoken in his own character, are those which have given, and which will continue to give, universal delight; and that the passages exclusively appropriate to the supposed narrator, such as the last couplet of the third stanza;[4] the seven last lines of the tenth; and the five following stanzas, with the exception of the four admirable lines at the commencement of the fourteenth, are felt by many unprejudiced and unsophisticated hearts, as sudden and unpleasant sinkings from the height to which the poet has previously lifted them, and to which he again re-elevates both himself and his reader.

If then I am compelled to doubt the theory by which the choice of *characters* was to be directed, not only *a priori,* from grounds of reason, but both from the few instances in which the poet himself *need* be supposed to have been governed by it, and from the comparative inferiority of those instances; still more must I hesitate in my assent to the sentence which immediately follows the former citation; and which I can neither admit as particular fact, nor as general rule. "The language too of these men is adopted (purified indeed from what appear to be its real defects, from all lasting and rational causes of dislike or disgust) because such men hourly communi-

---

"I've measured it from side to side;
'Tis three feet long, and two feet wide."

(C. quotes this couplet, and also the longer passages cited, from the text of 1815, which W. later altered)

cate with the best objects from which the best part of
language is originally derived; and because, from their
rank in society and the sameness and narrow circle of
their intercourse, being less under the action of social
vanity, they convey their feelings and notions in simple
and unelaborated expressions." To this I reply, that a rus-
tic's language, purified from all provincialism and gross-
ness, and so far reconstructed as to be made consistent
with the rules of grammar (which are in essence no other
than the laws of universal logic, applied to psychological
materials), will not differ from the language of any other
man of common-sense, however learned or refined he may
be, except as far as the notions, which the rustic has to
convey, are fewer and more indiscriminate. This will be-
come still clearer, if we add the consideration (equally im-
portant though less obvious) that the rustic, from the
more imperfect development of his faculties, and from
the lower state of their cultivation, aims almost solely to
convey *insulated facts,* either those of his scanty experi-
ence or his traditional belief; while the educated man
chiefly seeks to discover and express those *connections* of
things, or those relative *bearings* of fact to fact, from
which some more or less general law is deducible. For
facts are valuable to a wise man, chiefly as they lead to
the discovery of the indwelling *law* ·which is the true
being of things, the sole solution of their modes of exist-
ence, and in the knowledge of which consists our dignity
and our power.

As little can I agree with the assertion that from the
objects with which the rustic hourly communicates the
best part of language is formed. For first, if to com-
municate with' an object implies such an acquaintance
with it as renders it capable of being discriminately re-
flected on, the distinct knowledge of an uneducated rustic
would furnish a very scanty vocabulary. The few things
and modes of action requisite for his bodily conveniences,
would alone be individualized; while all the rest of nature
would be expressed by a small number of confused
general terms. Secondly, I deny that the words and com-
binations of words derived from the objects with which
the rustic is familiar, whether with distinct or confused
knowledge, can be justly said to form the *best* part of

language. It is more than probable that many classes of
the brute creation possess discriminating sounds by which
they can convey to each other notices of such objects as
concern their food, shelter, or safety. Yet we hesitate to
call the aggregate of such sounds a language, otherwise
than metaphorically. The best part of human language,
properly so called, is derived from reflection on the acts
of the mind itself. It is formed by a voluntary appropria-
tion of fixed symbols to internal acts, to processes and
results of imagination, the greater part of which have no
place in the consciousness of uneducated man; though in
civilized society, by imitation and passive remembrance
of what they hear from their religious instructors and
other superiors, the most uneducated share in the harvest
which they neither sowed nor reaped. If the history of the
phrases in hourly currency among our peasants were
traced, a person not previously aware of the fact would
be surprised at finding so large a number which three or
four centuries ago were the exclusive property of the
universities and the schools, and at the commencement of
the Reformation had been transferred from the school to
the pulpit, and thus gradually passed into common life.
The extreme difficulty, and often the impossibility, of
finding words for the simplest moral and intellectual
processes in the languages of uncivilized tribes has proved
perhaps the weightiest obstacle to the progress of our most
zealous and adroit missionaries. Yet these tribes are sur-
rounded by the same nature as our peasants are; but in
still more impressive forms; and they are, moreover,
obliged to *particularize* many more of them. When, there-
fore, Mr. Wordsworth adds, "accordingly, such a language"
(meaning, as before, the language of rustic life purified
from provincialism) "arising out of repeated experience
and regular feelings, is a more permanent, and a far more
philosophical language, than that which is frequently sub-
stituted for it by poets, who think they are conferring
honor upon themselves and their art in proportion as they
indulge in arbitrary and capricious habits of expression;"
it may be answered that the language which he has in
view can be attributed to rustics with no greater right
than the style of Hooker or Bacon to Tom Brown or Sir
Roger L'Estrange. Doubtless, if what is peculiar to each

were omitted in each, the result must needs be the same. Further, that the poet, who uses an illogical diction, or a style fitted to excite only the low and changeable pleasure of wonder by means of groundless novelty, substitutes a language of *folly* and *vanity*, not for that of the *rustic*, but for that of *good sense* and *natural feeling*.

Here let me be permitted to remind the reader that the positions which I controvert are contained in the sentences—*"a selection of the* REAL *language of men;"*— *"the language of these men"* (i.e. men in low and rustic life). *"I propose to myself to imitate, and, as far as possible, to adopt the very language of men." "Between the language of prose and that of metrical composition, there neither is nor can be any essential difference."* It is against these exclusively that my opposition is directed.

I object, in the very first instance, to an equivocation in the use of the word "real." Every man's language varies, according to the extent of his knowledge, the activity of his faculties, and the depth or quickness of his feelings. Every man's language has, first, its *individualities;* secondly, the common properties of the *class* to which he belongs; and thirdly, words and phrases of *universal* use. The language of Hooker, Bacon, Bishop Taylor, and Burke, differs from the common language of the learned class only by the superior number and novelty of the thoughts and relations which they had to convey. The language of Algernon Sidney differs not at all from that which every well-educated gentleman would wish to write, and (with due allowances for the undeliberateness, and less connected train, of thinking natural and proper to conversation) such as he would wish to talk. Neither one nor the other differ half as much from the general language of cultivated society as the language of Mr. Wordsworth's homeliest composition differs from that of a common peasant. For "real" therefore, we must substitute *ordinary*, or *lingua communis*. And this, we have proved, is no more to be found in the phraseology of low and rustic life than in that of any other class. Omit the peculiarities of each, and the result of course must be common to all. And assuredly the omissions and changes to be made in the language of rustics, before it could be transferred to any species of poem, except the drama or other professed imitation, are at least as numerous and weighty, as would be required in adapting to the same purpose the ordinary language of tradesmen and manufacturers. Not to mention that the language so highly extolled by Mr. Wordsworth varies in every county, nay in every village, according to the accidental character of the clergyman, the existence or nonexistence of schools; or even, perhaps, as the exciseman, publican, or barber, happen to be, or not to be, zealous politicians, and readers of the weekly newspaper *pro bono publico.* Anterior to cultivation, the *lingua communis* of every country, as Dante[5] has well observed, exists everywhere in parts, and nowhere as a whole.

Neither is the case rendered at all more tenable by the addition of the words *in a state of excitement.* For the nature of a man's words, when he is strongly affected by joy, grief, or anger, must necessarily depend on the number and quality of the general truths, conceptions, and images, and of the words expressing them, with which his mind had been previously stored. For the property of passion is not to *create;* but to set in increased activity. At least, whatever new connections of thoughts or images, or (which is equally, if not more than equally, the appropriate effect of strong excitement) whatever generalizations of truth or experience, the heat of passion may produce; yet the terms of their conveyance must have preexisted in his former conversations, and are only collected and crowded together by the unusual stimulation. It is indeed very possible to adopt in a poem the unmeaning repetitions, habitual phrases, and other blank counters, which an unfurnished or confused understanding interposes at short intervals, in order to keep hold of his subject, which is still slipping from him, and to give him time for recollection; or in mere aid of vacancy, as in the scanty companies of a country stage the same player pops backwards and forwards, in order to prevent the appearance of empty spaces, in the procession of *Macbeth,* or *Henry VIIIth.* But what assistance to the poet, or ornament to the poem, these can supply, I am at a loss to conjecture. Nothing assuredly can differ either in origin or in mode

[5] Dante *De vulgari eloquentia,* I, xvi

more widely from the *apparent* tautologies of intense and turbulent feeling, in which the passion is greater and of longer endurance than to be exhausted or satisfied by a single representation of the image or incident exciting it. Such repetitions I admit to be a beauty of the highest kind; as illustrated by Mr. Wordsworth himself from the song of Deborah.[6] "*At her feet he bowed, he fell, he lay down; at her feet he bowed, he fell; where he bowed, there he fell down dead.*"

Chapter XVIII

Language of metrical composition, why and wherein essentially different from that of prose—Origin and elements of metre—Its necessary consequences, and the conditions thereby imposed on the metrical writer in the choice of his diction.

I CONCLUDE, therefore, that the attempt is impracticable; and that, were it not impracticable, it would still be useless. For the very power of making the selection implies the previous possession of the language selected. Or where can the poet have lived? And by what rules could he direct his choice, which would not have enabled him to select and arrange his words by the light of his own judgment? We do not adopt the language of a class by the mere adoption of such words exclusively, as that class would use, or at least understand; but likewise by following the *order* in which the words of such men are wont to succeed each other. Now this order, in the intercourse of uneducated men, is distinguished from the diction of their superiors in knowledge and power, by the greater *disjunction* and *separation* in the component parts of that, whatever it be, which they wish to communicate. There is a want of that prospectiveness of mind, that *surview,* which enables a man to foresee the whole of what he is to convey, appertaining to any one point; and by this means so to subordinate and arrange the different parts according to their relative importance, as to convey it at once, and as an organized whole.

[6] Deborah W. quotes Judges, V, 27 (note to "The Thorn")

Now I will take the first stanza on which I have
chanced to open in the Lyrical Ballads. It is one the
most simple and the least peculiar in its language.

> In distant countries have I been,
> And yet I have not often seen
> A healthy man, a man full grown,
> Weep in the public roads alone.
> But such a one, on English ground,
> And in the broad highway, I met;
> Along the broad highway he came,
> His cheeks with tears were wet.
> Sturdy he seemed, though he was sad;
> And in his arms a lamb he had.[1]

The words here are doubtless such as are current in all
ranks of life; and of course not less so in the hamlet and
cottage than in the shop, manufactory, college, or palace.
But is this the *order* in which the rustic would have placed
the words? I am grievously deceived if the following less
compact mode of commencing the same tale be not a far
more faithful copy. "I have been in a many parts far and
near, and I don't know that I ever saw before a man
crying by himself in the public road; a grown man I mean,
that was neither sick nor hurt," &c., &c. But when I turn
to the following stanza in "The Thorn":

> At all times of the day and night
> This wretched woman thither goes,
> And she is known to every star,
> And every wind that blows;
> And there beside the thorn she sits,
> When the blue day-light's in the skies;
> And when the whirlwind's on the hill,
> Or frosty air is keen and still;
> And to herself she cries,
> Oh misery! Oh misery!
> Oh woe is me! Oh misery!

and compare this with the language of ordinary men; or
with that which I can conceive at all likely to proceed,
in *real* life, from *such* a narrator, as is supposed in the
note to the poem; compare it either in the succession of
the images or of the sentences; I am reminded of the

[1] had "The Last of the Flock"

sublime prayer and hymn of praise which MILTON,[2] in opposition to an established liturgy, presents as a fair *specimen* of common extemporary devotion, and such as we might expect to hear from every self-inspired minister of a conventicle! And I reflect with delight how little a mere theory, though of his own workmanship, interferes with the processes of genuine imagination in a man of true poetic genius, who possesses, as Mr. Wordsworth, if ever man did, most assuredly does possess,

"THE VISION AND THE FACULTY DIVINE." [3]

One point then alone remains, but that the most important; its examination having been, indeed, my chief inducement for the preceding inquisition. *"There neither is nor can be any essential difference between the language of prose and metrical composition."* Such is Mr. Wordsworth's assertion. Now prose itself, at least in all argumentative and consecutive works, differs, and ought to differ, from the language of conversation; even as reading ought to differ from talking.[4] Unless therefore the difference denied be that of the mere *words,* as materials common to all styles of writing, and not of the *style*[5] itself in the universally admitted sense of the term, it might be naturally presumed that there must exist a still greater between the ordonnance of poetic composition and that of prose than is expected to distinguish prose from ordinary conversation.

There are not, indeed, examples wanting in the history of literature of apparent paradoxes that have summoned the public wonder as new and startling truths, but which on examination have shrunk into tame and harmless *truisms;* as the eyes of a cat, seen in the dark, have been mistaken for flames of fire. But Mr. Wordsworth is

[2] **MILTON** *Paradise Lost,* V, 144, etc.

[3] **DIVINE** quoted from W.'s poem, *The Excursion,* I, 79. Since what precedes belongs logically to the preceding chapter, ch. XVIII should begin after this line.

[4] **talking** here C. prints a long note against teaching children to read as they would talk.

[5] **words . . . style** the Oxford and Cambridge editors of *Biog. Lit.* both argue that W. meant merely words, but Abrams, Barstow, and Owen say style. See Bibliography.

among the last men to whom a delusion of this kind would
be attributed by anyone who had enjoyed the slightest
opportunity of understanding his mind and character.
Where an objection has been anticipated by such an
author as natural, his answer to it must needs be in-
terpreted in some sense which either is, or has been, or
is capable of being controverted. My object then must
be to discover some other meaning for the term *essential
difference* in this place, exclusive of the indistinction and
community of the words themselves. For whether there
ought to exist a class of words in the English in any
degree resembling the poetic dialect of the Greek and
Italian, is a question of very subordinate importance. The
number of such words would be small indeed in our
language; and even in the Italian and Greek, they con-
sist not so much of different words, as of slight differences
in the *forms* of declining and conjugating the same words;
forms, doubtless, which having been, at some period more
or less remote, the common grammatic flexions of some
tribe or province, had been accidentally appropriated to
poetry by the general admiration of certain master intel-
lects, the first established lights of inspiration, to whom
that dialect happened to be native.

Essence, in its primary signification, means the principle
of *individuation*, the inmost principle of the *possibility* of
any thing, *as* that particular thing. It is equivalent to the
idea of a thing, whenever we use the word *idea* with
philosophic precision. Existence, on the other hand, is
distinguished from essence, by the superinduction of
reality. Thus we speak of the essence, and essential prop-
erties of a circle; but we do not therefore assert, that any
thing, which really *exists*, is mathematically circular. Thus
too, without any tautology we contend for the *existence*
of the Supreme Being; that is, for a reality correspondent
to the idea. There is, next, a *secondary* use of the word
essence, in which it signifies the point or ground of con-
tra-distinction between two modifications of the same sub-
stance or subject. Thus we should be allowed to say that
the style of architecture of Westminster Abbey is *essen-
tially* different from that of St. Paul's, even though both
had been built with blocks cut into the same form, and
from the same quarry. Only in this latter sense of the term

must it have been *denied* by Mr. Wordsworth (for in this sense alone is it *affirmed* by the general opinion) that the language of poetry (i.e. the formal construction, or architecture, of the words and phrases) is *essentially* different from that of prose. Now the burthen of the proof lies with the oppugner, not with the supporters of the common belief. Mr. Wordsworth, in consequence, assigns as the proof of his position "that not only the language of a large portion of every good poem, even of the most elevated character, must necessarily, except with reference to the metre, in no respect differ from that of good prose, but likewise that some of the most interesting parts of the best poems will be found to be strictly the language of prose, when prose is well written. The truth of this assertion might be demonstrated by innumerable passages from almost all the poetical writings even of Milton himself." He then quotes Gray's sonnet—

> In vain to me the smiling mornings shine,
> And reddening Phoebus lifts his golden fire;
> The birds in vain their amorous descant join,
> Or cheerful fields resume their green attire.
> These ears, alas! for other notes repine;
> *A different object do these eyes require;*
> *My lonely anguish melts no heart but mine;*
> *And in my breast the imperfect joys expire.*
> Yet morning smiles the busy race to cheer,
> And newborn pleasure brings to happier men:
> The fields to all their wonted tribute bear,
> To warm their little loves the birds complain.
> *I fruitless mourn to him that cannot hear,*
> *And weep the more because I weep in vain,*

and adds the following remark:—"It will easily be perceived, that the only part of this Sonnet which is of any value is the lines printed in italics. It is equally obvious, that, except in the rhyme, and in the use of the single word 'fruitless' for 'fruitlessly,' which is so far a defect, the language of these lines does in no respect differ from that of prose."

An idealist defending his system by the fact that when asleep we often believe ourselves awake, was well answered by his plain neighbor, "Ah, but when awake do we ever believe ourselves asleep?"—Things identical must be convertible. The preceding passage seems to rest on a similar sophism. For the question is not whether there may not occur in prose an order of words which would be equally proper in a poem; nor whether there are not beautiful lines and sentences of frequent occurrence in good poems which would be equally becoming as well as beautiful in good prose; for neither the one nor the other has ever been either denied or doubted by any one. The true question must be whether there are not modes of expression, a *construction*, and an *order* of sentences, which are in their fit and natural place in a serious prose composition, but would be disproportionate and hetero-geneous in metrical poetry; and, *vice versa,* whether in the language of a serious poem there may not be an arrangement both of words and sentences, and a use and selection of (what are called) *figures of speech,* both as to their kind, their frequency, and their occasions, which on a subject of equal weight would be vicious and alien in correct and manly prose. I contend that in both cases this unfitness of each for the place of the other frequently will and ought to exist.

And first from the *origin* of metre. This I would trace to the balance in the mind effected by that spontaneous effort which strives to hold in check the workings of pas-sion. It might be easily explained likewise in what manner this salutary antagonism is assisted by the very state which it counteracts; and how this balance of antagonists became organized into *metre* (in the usual acceptation of that term) by a supervening act of the will and judgment, consciously and for the foreseen purpose of pleasure. Assuming these principles as the data of our argument, we deduce from them two legitimate conditions, which the critic is entitled to expect in every metrical work. First, that as the *elements* of metre owe their existence to a state of increased excitement, so the metre itself should be accompanied by the natural language of excitement. Secondly, that as these elements are formed into metre *artificially,* by a *voluntary* act, with the design and for the purpose of blending *delight* with emotion, so the traces of present *volition* should throughout the metrical language be proportionally discernible. Now these two conditions must be reconciled and co-present. There must be not only a partnership, but a union; an interpenetration of passion and of will, of *spontaneous* impulse and of *voluntary* purpose. Again, this union can be manifested only in a frequency of forms and figures of speech (originally the offspring of passion, but now the adopted children of power) greater than would be desired or endured where the emotion is not voluntarily encouraged and kept up for the sake of that pleasure which such emotion, so tempered and mastered by the will, is found capable of communicating. It not only dictates, but of itself tends to produce, a more frequent employment of picturesque and vivifying language than would be natural in any other case in which there did not exist, as there does in the present, a previous and well understood, though tacit, *compact* between the poet and his reader, that the latter is entitled to expect, and the former bound to supply, this species and degree of pleasurable excitement. We may in some measure apply to this union the answer of POLIXENES, in the *Winter's Tale*,[6] to PERDITA's neglect of the streaked gilly-flowers, because she had heard it said,

> There is an art which, in their piedness, shares
> With great creating nature.
>   *Pol:* Say there be;
> Yet nature is made better by no mean,
> But nature makes that mean; so ev'n that art
> Which you say adds to nature, is an art,
> That nature makes. You see, sweet maid, we marry
> *A gentler scion to the wildest stock;*
> And make conceive a bark of ruder kind
> By bud of nobler race. This is an art,
> Which does mend nature—change it rather; but
> The art itself is nature.

Secondly, I argue from the EFFECTS [7] of metre. As far as metre acts in and for itself, it tends to increase the vivacity and susceptibility both of the general feelings and of the attention. This effect it produces by the continued

[6] Winter's Tale IV, iv, 87-97
[7] EFFECTS to support his thesis that the language of poetry and prose must differ, C. first considers the poet. In his second point, he turns to the effect of a poem on the reader, and in his third and fourth points to the poem itself, related to the passion of the poet, and to the object of imitation.

excitement of surprise, and by the quick reciprocations of curiosity still gratified and still re-excited, which are too slight indeed to be at any one moment objects of distinct consciousness, yet become considerable in their aggregate influence. As a medicated atmosphere, or as wine during animated conversation, they act powerfully, though themselves unnoticed. Where, therefore, correspondent food and appropriate matter are not provided for the attention and feelings thus roused, there must needs be a disappointment felt; like that of leaping in the dark from the last step of a stair-case, when we had prepared our muscles for a leap of three or four.

The discussion on the powers of metre in the preface is highly ingenious and touches at all points on truth. But I cannot find any statement of its powers considered abstractly and separately. On the contrary Mr. Wordsworth seems always to estimate metre by the powers which it exerts during (and, as I think, in *consequence of*) its combination with other elements of poetry. Thus the previous difficulty is left unanswered, *what* the elements are with which it must be combined in order to produce its own effects to any pleasurable purpose. Double and tri-syllable rhymes, indeed, form a lower species of wit, and attended to exclusively for their own sake, may become a source of momentary amusement; as in poor Smart's distich[8] to the Welsh squire who had promised him a hare:

> Tell me, thou son of great Cadwallader!
> Hast sent the hare? or hast thou swallow'd her?

But for any *poetic* purposes, metre resembles (if the aptness of the simile may excuse its meanness) yeast, worthless or disagreeable by itself, but giving vivacity and spirit to the liquor with which it is proportionately combined.

The reference to the "Children in the Wood" by no means satisfies my judgment. We all willingly throw ourselves back for awhile into the feelings of our childhood. This ballad, therefore, we read under such recollections

---

[8] distich C. slightly misquotes Christopher Smart, "To the Rev. Mr. Powell"

of our own childish feelings as would equally endear to
us poems which Mr. Wordsworth himself would regard as
faulty in the opposite extreme of gaudy and technical
ornament. Before the invention of printing, and in a still
greater degree, before the introduction of writing, metre,
especially *alliterative* metre (whether alliterative at the
beginning of the words, as in "Pierce Plouman," or at the
end as in rhymes) possessed an independent value as
assisting the recollection, and consequently the preserva-
tion, of *any* series of truths or incidents. But I am not
convinced by the collation of facts that the "Children in
the Wood" owes either its preservation or its popularity,
to its metrical form. Mr. Marshal's repository[9] affords a
number of tales in prose inferior in pathos and general
merit, some of as old a date, and many as widely popular.
"TOM HICKATHRIFT," "JACK THE GIANT-KILLER,"
"GOODY TWO-SHOES," and "LITTLE RED RIDING-
HOOD" are formidable rivals. And that they have con-
tinued in prose cannot be fairly explained by the assump-
tion that the comparative meanness of their thoughts and
images precluded even the humblest forms of metre. The
scene of GOODY TWO-SHOES in the church is perfectly
susceptible of metrical narration; and among the Θαύματα
θαυμαστότατα[10] even of the present age, I do not recollect
a more astonishing image than that of the *"whole rookery,
that flew out of the giant's beard,"* scared by the tre-
mendous voice with which this monster answered the
challenge of the heroic TOM HICKATHRIFT!

If from these we turn to compositions universally, and
independently of all early associations, beloved and
admired; would "THE MARIA," "THE MONK," or "THE
POOR MAN'S ASS" of STERNE,[11] be read with more
delight, or have a better chance of immortality, had they
without any change in the diction been composed in
rhyme, than in their present state? If I am not grossly
mistaken, the general reply would be in the negative.
Nay, I will confess that in Mr. Wordsworth's own volumes,
the "ANECDOTE FOR FATHERS," "SIMON LEE,"
"ALICE FELL," "THE BEGGARS," and "THE SAIL-

[9] **repository** apparently a bookshop
[10] θαυμαστότατα marvels most marvellous
[11] **STERNE** stories from *A Sentimental Journey*

OR'S MOTHER," notwithstanding the beauties which are
to be found in each of them where the poet interposes the
music of his own thoughts, would have been more de-
lightful to me in prose, told and managed, as by Mr.
Wordsworth they would have been, in a moral essay, or
pedestrian tour.

Metre in itself is simply a stimulant of the attention,
and therefore excites the question: Why is the attention to
be thus stimulated? Now the question cannot be answered
by the pleasure of the metre itself: for this we have shown
to be *conditional,* and dependent on the appropriateness
of the thoughts and expressions to which the metrical form
is superadded. Neither can I conceive any other answer
that can be rationally given, short of this: I write in metre,
because I am about to use a language different from that
of prose. Besides, where the language is not such, how
interesting soever the reflections are that are capable of
being drawn by a philosophic mind from the thoughts or
incidents of the poem, the metre itself must often become
feeble. Take the three last stanzas of "THE SAILOR'S
MOTHER," for instance. If I could for a moment abstract
from the effect produced on the author's feelings, as a
man, by the incident at the time of its real occurrence, I
would dare appeal to his own judgment, whether in the
metre itself he found a sufficient reason for *their* being
written *metrically?*

> And thus continuing, she said,
> I had a son, who many a day
> Sailed on the seas; but he is dead;
> In Denmark he was cast away:
> And I have travelled far as Hull, to see
> What clothes he might have left, or other property.
>
> The bird and cage, they both were his;
> 'Twas my son's bird; and neat and trim
> He kept it: many voyages
> His singing-bird hath gone with him;
> When last he sailed he left the bird behind;
> As it might be, perhaps, from bodings of his mind.
>
> He to a fellow-lodger's care
> Had left it, to be watched and fed,
> Till he came back again; and there
> I found it when my son was dead;

> And now, God help me for my little wit!
> I trail it with me, Sir! he took so much delight in it.[12]

If disproportioning the emphasis we read these stanzas so as to make the rhymes perceptible, even *tri-syllable* rhymes could scarcely produce an equal sense of oddity and strangeness as we feel here in finding *rhymes at all* in sentences so exclusively colloquial. I would further ask whether, but for that visionary state into which the figure of the woman and the susceptibility of his own genius had placed the poet's imagination (a state which spreads its influence and coloring over all that co-exists with the exciting cause, and in which

"The simplest, and the most familiar things
  Gain a strange power of spreading awe around them"),[13]

I would ask the poet whether he would not have felt an abrupt downfall in these verses from the preceding stanza?

> The ancient spirit is not dead;
> Old times, thought I, are breathing there;
> Proud was I that my country bred
> Such strength, a dignity so fair:
> She begged an alms, like one in poor estate;
> I looked at her again, nor did my pride abate.

It must not be omitted, and is besides worthy of notice, that those stanzas furnish the only fair instance that I have been able to discover in all Mr. Wordsworth's writings of an *actual* adoption, or true imitation, of the *real* and *very* language of *low and rustic life,* freed from provincialisms.

Thirdly, I deduce the position from all the causes elsewhere assigned, which render metre the proper form of poetry, and poetry imperfect and defective without metre. Metre, therefore, having been connected with *poetry* most often and by a peculiar fitness, whatever else is combined with *metre* must, though it be not itself *essentially* poetic, have nevertheless some property in common with poetry, as an intermedium of affinity, a sort (if I may dare borrow a well-known phrase from technical

[12] it text of 1815, later altered by W.
[13] them altered from the description of Night-mair in the *Remorse* (C.'s note, shortened. *Remorse* is his tragedy).

chemistry) of *mordant*[14] between it and the superadded
metre. Now poetry, Mr. Wordsworth truly affirms, does
always imply PASSION: which word must be here under-
stood in its most general sense, as an excited state of the
feelings and faculties. And as every passion has its proper
pulse, so will it likewise have its characteristic modes of
expression. But where there exists that degree of genius
and talent which entitles a writer to aim at the honors of
a poet, the very *act* of poetic composition *itself* is, and is
allowed to imply and to produce, an unusual state of
excitement, which of course justifies and demands a cor-
respondent difference of language, as truly, though not
perhaps in as marked a degree, as the excitement of love,
fear, rage, or jealousy. The vividness of the descriptions or
declamations in DONNE or DRYDEN is as much and as
often derived from the force and fervor of the describer,
as from the reflections, forms, or incidents which con-
stitute their subject and materials. The wheels take fire
from the mere rapidity of their motion. To what extent,
and under what modifications, this may be admitted to
act, I shall attempt to define in an after remark[15] on Mr.
Wordsworth's reply to this objection, or rather on his ob-
jection to this reply, as already anticipated in his preface.

Fourthly, and as intimately connected with this, if not
the same argument in a more general form, I adduce the
high spiritual instinct of the human being impelling us to
seek unity by harmonious adjustment, and thus establish-
ing the principle that *all* the parts of an organized whole
must be assimilated to the more *important* and *essential*
parts. This and the preceding arguments may be strength-
ened by the reflection that the composition of a poem is
among the *imitative* arts; and that imitation, as opposed
to copying, consists either in the interfusion of the SAME
throughout the radically DIFFERENT, or of the different
throughout a base radically the same.

Lastly, I appeal to the practice of the best poets, of all
countries and in all ages, as *authorizing* the opinion (*de-
duced* from all the foregoing) that in every import of the
word ESSENTIAL, which would not here involve a mere
truism, there may be, is, and ought to be, an *essential*

[14] **mordant** a fixative for dyes
[15] **remark** see note 20 below

difference between the language of prose and of metrical
composition.

In Mr. Wordsworth's criticism of GRAY's Sonnet, the
reader's sympathy with his praise or blame of the differ-
ent parts is taken for granted rather perhaps too easily. He
has not, at least, attempted to win or compel it by argu-
mentative analysis. In *my* conception at least, the lines
rejected as of no value do, with the exception of the two
first, differ as much and as little from the language of
common life, as those which he has printed in italics as
possessing genuine excellence. Of the five lines thus
honorably distinguished, two of them differ from prose
even more widely than the lines which either precede or
follow, in the *position* of the words.

> *A different object do these eyes require;*
> My lonely anguish melts no heart but mine;
> *And in my breast the imperfect joys expire.*

But were it otherwise, what would this prove but a
truth of which no man ever doubted? Videlicet, that there
are sentences which would be equally in their place both
in verse and prose. Assuredly it does not prove the point
which alone requires proof; namely, that there are not
passages which would suit the one and not suit the other.
The first line of this sonnet is distinguished from the
ordinary language of men by the epithet to morning. (For
we will set aside, at present, the consideration, that the
particular word "*smiling*" is hackneyed and (as it involves
a sort of personification) not quite congruous with the
common and material attribute of *shining*.) And, doubt-
less, this adjunction of epithets for the purpose of addi-
tional description, where no particular attention is de-
manded for the quality of the thing, would be noticed as
giving a poetic cast to a man's conversation. Should the
sportsman exclaim, "*Come boys! the rosy morning calls
you up,*" he will be supposed to have some song in his
head. But no one suspects this, when he says, "A wet
morning shall not confine us to our beds." This then is
either a defect in poetry, or it is not. Whoever should
decide in the *affirmative*, I would request him to re-peruse
any one poem of any confessedly great poet from Homer
to Milton, or from Aeschylus to Shakespeare; and to strike

out (in thought I mean) every instance of this kind. If the number of these fancied erasures did not startle him; or if he continued to deem the work improved by their total omission; he must advance reasons of no ordinary strength and evidence, reasons grounded in the essence of human nature. Otherwise, I should not hesitate to consider him as a man not so much *proof against* all authority, as *dead to it.*

The second line,

"And reddening Phoebus lifts his golden fire;" has indeed almost as many faults as words. But then it is a bad line, not because the language is distinct from that of prose; but because it conveys incongruous images, because it confounds the cause and the effect, the real *thing* with the personified *representative* of the thing; in short, because it differs from the language of GOOD SENSE! That the "Phoebus" is hackneyed, and a schoolboy image, is an *accidental* fault, dependent on the age in which the author wrote, and not deduced from the nature of the thing. That it is part of an exploded mythology is an objection more deeply grounded. Yet when the torch of ancient learning was re-kindled, so cheering were its beams that our eldest poets, cut off by Christianity from all *accredited* machinery, and deprived of all *acknowledged* guardians and symbols of the great objects of nature,[16] were naturally induced to adopt, as a *poetic* language, those fabulous personages, those forms of the supernatural in nature, which had given them such dear delight in the poems of their great masters. Nay, even at this day what scholar of genial taste will not so far sympathize with them as to read with pleasure in PETRARCH, CHAUCER, or SPENSER, what he would perhaps condemn as puerile in a modern poet?

I remember no poet whose writings would safelier stand the test of Mr. Wordsworth's theory than SPENSER. Yet will Mr. Wordsworth say that the style of the following stanzas is either undistinguished from prose, and the

---

[16] But still more by the mechanical system of philosophy which has needlessly infected our theological opinions, and teaching us to consider the world in its relation to God, as of a building to its mason, leaves the idea of omnipresence a mere abstract notion in the state-room of our reason (C.'s note).

language of ordinary life? Or that it is vicious, and that the stanzas are *blots* in the "Faery Queen"?

> By this the northern waggoner had set
> His sevenfold teme behind the stedfast starre,
> That was in ocean waves yet never wet,
> But firme is fixt, and sendeth light from farre
> To all that in the wild deep wandering are:
> And chearful chanticleer with his note shrill
> Had warned once that Phoebus' fiery carre
> In haste was climbing up the easterne hill,
> Full envious that night so long his roome did fill.
>
> *Book* I. *Can.* 2. *St.* 1

> At last the golden orientall gate
> Of greatest heaven gan to open fayre,
> And Phoebus fresh, as brydegrome to his mate,
> Came dauncing forth, shaking his deawie hayre,
> And hurl'd his glist'ring beams through gloomy ayre:
> Which when the wakeful elfe perceived, streightway
> He started up, and did him selfe prepayre
> In sun-bright armes and battailous array;
> For with that pagan proud he combat will that day.
>
> *Book* I. *Can.* 5. *St.* 2.

On the contrary to how many passages, both in hymn books and in blank verse poems, could I (were it not invidious) direct the reader's attention, the style of which is most *unpoetic, because,* and only because, it is the style of *prose?* He will not suppose me capable of having in my mind such verses as

> I put my hat upon my head
> And walk'd into the Strand;
> And there I met another man,
> Whose hat was in his hand.[17]

To such specimens it would indeed be a fair and full reply that these lines are not bad because they are *unpoetic;* but because they are empty of all sense and feeling; and that it were an idle attempt to prove that an ape is not a Newton, when it is evident that he is not a man. But the sense shall be good and weighty, the language correct and dignified, the subject interesting and treated with feeling; and yet the style shall, notwith-

[17] hand Dr. Johnson's parody, quoted by W. in the Preface

standing all these merits, be justly blamable as *prosaic*, and solely because the words and the order of the words would find their appropriate place in prose, but are not suitable to *metrical* composition. The "Civil Wars" of Daniel is an instructive, and even interesting work; but take the following stanzas (and from the hundred instances which abound I might probably have selected others far more striking):

> And to the end we may with better ease
> Discern the true discourse, vouchsafe to shew
> What were the times foregoing near to these,
> That these we may with better profit know:
> Tell how the world fell into this disease;
> And how so great distemperature did grow;
> So shall we see with what degrees it came;
> How things at full do soon wax out of frame.
>
> Ten kings had from the Norman conqu'ror reign'd
> With intermixt and variable fate,
> When England to her greatest height attain'd
> Of power, dominion, glory, wealth, and state;
> After it had with much ado sustain'd
> The violence of princes, with debate
> For titles and the often mutinies
> Of nobles for their ancient liberties.
>
> For first, the Norman, conqu'ring all by might,
> By might was forced to keep what he had got;
> Mixing our customs and the form of right
> With foreign constitutions he had brought;
> Mastering the mighty, humbling the poorer wight,
> By all severest means that could be wrought;
> And, making the succession doubtful, rent
> His new-got state, and left it turbulent.
>
> *B. I. St. VII. VIII. & IX.*

Will it be contended, on the one side, that these lines are mean and senseless? Or on the other, that they are not prosaic, and for *that* reason unpoetic? This poet's well-merited epithet is that of the *"well-languaged* [18] *Daniel"*; but likewise, and by the consent of his contemporaries no less than of all succeeding critics, the "prosaic Daniel." Yet those who thus designate this wise and amiable

[18] **well-languaged** epithet from William Browne's *Britannia's Pastorals* II, ii, 303

writer, from the frequent incorrespondency of his diction
to his metre in the majority of his compositions, not only
deem them valuable and interesting on other accounts;
but willingly admit that there are to be found throughout
his poems, and especially in his *Epistles* and in his
Hymen's Triumph, many and exquisite specimens of that
style which, as the *neutral ground* of prose and verse, is
common to both. A fine and almost faultless extract,
eminent, as for other beauties, so for its perfection in this
species of diction, may be seen in LAMB'S *Dramatic
Specimens,* &c., a work of various interest from the nature
of the selections themselves (all from the plays of
Shakespeare's contemporaries), and deriving a high addi-
tional value from the notes, which are full of just and
original criticism, expressed with all the freshness of
originality.

Among the possible effects of practical adherence to
a theory that aims to *identify* the style of prose and verse
(if it does not indeed claim for the latter a yet nearer
resemblance to the average style of men in the *viva voce*
intercourse of real life) we might anticipate the following
as not the least likely to occur. It will happen, as I have
indeed before observed, that the metre itself, the sole
acknowledged difference, will occasionally become metre
to the eye only. The existence of *prosaisms,* and that they
detract from the merit of a poem, *must* at length be con-
ceded, when a number of successive lines can be rendered,
even to the most delicate ear, unrecognizable as verse, or
as having even been intended for verse, by simply tran-
scribing them as prose; when, if the poem be in blank verse,
this can be effected without any alteration, or at most by
merely restoring one or two words to their proper places,
from which they have been transplanted for no assignable
cause or reason but that of the author's convenience; [19] but,
if it be in rhyme, by the mere exchange of the final word
of each line for some other of the same meaning, equally
appropriate, dignified, and euphonic.

The answer or objection in the preface to the an-
ticipated remark "that metre paves the way to other dis-

---

[19] As the ingenious gentleman under the influence of the Tragic
Muse contrived to dislocate, "I wish you a good morning, Sir!

tinctions," is contained in the following[20] words. "The distinction of rhyme and metre is voluntary and uniform, and not, like that produced by (what is called) poetic diction, arbitrary, and subject to infinite caprices, upon which no calculation whatever can be made. In the one case the reader is utterly at the mercy of the poet respecting what imagery or diction he may choose to connect with the passion." But is this a *poet*, of whom a poet is speaking? No, surely! rather of a fool or madman: or at

---

Thank you, Sir, and I wish you the same," into two blank-verse heroics:—

"To you a morning good, good Sir! I wish.
You, Sir! I thank: to you the same wish I."

In those parts of Mr. Wordsworth's works which I have thoroughly studied, I find fewer instances in which this would be practicable than I have met in many poems where an approximation of prose has been sedulously and on system guarded against. Indeed excepting the stanzas already quoted from "THE SAILOR'S MOTHER," I can recollect but one instance: viz., a short passage of four or five lines in "THE BROTHERS," that model of English pastoral, which I have never yet read with unclouded eye.—"James, pointing to its summit, over which they had all purposed to return together, informed them that he would wait for them *there*. They parted, and his comrades passed that way some two hours after, but they did not find him at the appointed place, *a circumstance of which they took no heed:* but one of them, going by chance into the house, which at this time was James's house, learnt *there*, that nobody had seen him all that day." The only change which has been made is in the position of the little word *there* in two instances, the position in the original being clearly such as is not adopted in ordinary conversation. The other words printed in *italics* were so marked because, though good and genuine English, they are not the phraseology of common conversation either in the word put in apposition, or in the connection by the genitive pronoun. Men in general would have said, "but that was a circumstance they paid no attention to, or took no notice of," and the language is, on the theory of the preface, justified only by the narrator's being the *Vicar*. Yet if any ear *could* suspect, that these sentences were ever printed as metre, on those very words alone could the suspicion have been grounded. (C. quotes the text of 1800, not quite accurately)
[20] **following** see n. 15 above. The "following words" follow immediately only in the text of the Preface of 1800.

best of a vain or ignorant phantast! And might not brains
so wild and so deficient make just the same havoc with
rhymes and metres as they are supposed to effect with
modes and figures of speech? How is the reader at the
mercy of such men? If he continue to read their nonsense,
is it not his own fault? The ultimate end of criticism is
much more to establish the principles of writing than to
furnish *rules* how to pass judgment on what has been
written by others; if indeed it were possible that the two
could be separated. But if it be asked, by what principles
the poet is to regulate his own style, if he do not adhere
closely to the sort and order of words which he hears in
the market, wake, high-road, or plough-field? I reply, by
principles, the ignorance or neglect of which would con-
vict him of being no *poet,* but a silly or presumptuous
usurper of the name! By the principles of grammar, logic,
psychology! In one word by such a knowledge of the
facts, material and spiritual, that most appertain to his
art, as, if it have been governed and applied by *good sense,*
and rendered instinctive by habit, becomes the representa-
tive and reward of our past conscious reasonings, insights,
and conclusions, and acquires the name of TASTE. By
what *rule* that does not leave the reader at the poet's
mercy, and the poet at his own, is the latter to dis-
tinguish between the language suitable to *suppressed,* and
the language which is characteristic of *indulged,* anger?
Or between that of rage and that of jealousy? Is it obtained
by wandering about in search of angry or jealous people
in uncultivated society, in order to copy their words? Or
not far rather by the power of imagination proceeding
upon the *all in each* of human nature? By *meditation,*
rather than by *observation?* And by the latter in conse-
quence only of the former? As eyes, for which the former
has pre-determined their field of vision, and to which, as
to *its* organ, it communicates a microscopic power? There
is not, I firmly believe, a man now living, who has from
his own inward experience a clearer intuition, than Mr.
Wordsworth himself, that the last mentioned are the true
sources of *genial* discrimination. Through the same process
and by the same creative agency will the poet distinguish
the degree and kind of the excitement produced by the
very act of poetic composition. As intuitively will he know

what differences of style it at once inspires and justifies; what intermixture of conscious volition is natural to that state; and in what instances such figures and colors of speech degenerate into mere creatures of an arbitrary purpose, cold technical artifices of ornament or connection. For even as truth is its own light and evidence, discovering at once itself and falsehood, so is it the prerogative of poetic genius to distinguish by parental instinct its proper offspring from the changelings which the gnomes of vanity or the fairies of fashion may have laid in its cradle or called by its names. Could a rule be given from *without*, poetry would cease to be poetry, and sink into a mechanical art. It would be μόρφωσις, not ποίησις.[21] The *rules* of the IMAGINATION are themselves the very powers of growth and production. The *words* to which they are reducible present only the outlines and external appearance of the fruit. A deceptive counterfeit of the superficial form and colors may be elaborated; but the marble peach feels cold and heavy, and *children* only put it to their mouths. We find no difficulty in admitting as excellent, and the legitimate language of poetic fervor self-impassioned, DONNE'S apostrophe to the Sun in the second stanza of his "Progress of the Soul":

Thee, eye of heaven! this great soul envies not:
By thy male force is all we have begot.
In the first East thou now beginn'st to shine,
Suck'st early balm and island spices there,
And wilt anon in thy loose-rein'd career
At Tagus, Po, Seine, Thames, and Danow dine,
And see at night this western world of mine:
Yet hast thou not more nations seen than she,
Who before thee one day began to be,
And, thy frail light being quench'd, shall long, long outlive
    thee!

Or the next stanza but one:

Great destiny, the commissary of God,
That hast mark'd out a path and period
For ev'ry thing! Who, where we offspring took,
Our ways and ends see'st at one instant: thou
Knot of all causes! Thou, whose changeless brow

[21] ποίησις fashioning, not creation

Ne'er smiles or frowns! O! vouchsafe thou to look,
And shew my story in thy eternal book, &c.

As little difficulty do we find in excluding from the
honors of unaffected warmth and elevation the madness
prepense of pseudo-poesy, or the startling *hysteric* of
weakness over-exerting itself, which bursts on the unpre-
pared reader in sundry odes and apostrophes to abstract
terms. Such are the Odes to Jealousy, to Hope, to Oblivion,
and the like, in Dodsley's collection and the magazines
of that day, which seldom fail to remind me of an Oxford
copy of verses on the two SUTTONS, commencing with

"INOCULATION, heavenly maid! descend!" [22]

It is not to be denied that men of undoubted talents,
and even poets of true though not of first-rate genius,
have from a mistaken theory deluded both themselves and
others in the opposite extreme. I once read to a company
of sensible and well-educated women the introductory
period of Cowley's preface to his *"Pindaric Odes, written
in imitation of the style and manner of the odes of
Pindar."* "If (says Cowley) a man should undertake to
translate Pindar word for word, it would be thought that
one man had translated another; as may appear, when
he, that understands not the original, reads the verbal
traduction of him into Latin prose, than which nothing
seems more raving." I then proceeded with his own free
version of the second Olympic, composed for the charita-
ble purpose of *rationalizing* the Theban Eagle.

> Queen of all harmonious things,
> Dancing words and speaking strings,
> What God, what hero, wilt thou sing?
> What happy man to equal glories bring?
> Begin, begin thy noble choice,
> And let the hills around reflect the image of thy voice.
> Pisa does to Jove belong,
> Jove and Pisa claim thy song.
> The fair first-fruits of war, th' Olympic games,
> Alcides offer'd up to Jove;
> Alcides too thy strings may move!
> But oh! what man to join with these can worthy prove?

[22] descend *Gentleman's Magazine,* October, 1783 (vol. LIII, p. 869)

Join Theron boldly to their sacred names;
Theron the next honor claims;
Theron to no man gives place,
Is first in Pisa's and in Virtue's race;
Theron there, and he alone,
Ev'n his own swift forefathers has outgone.

One of the company exclaimed, with the full assent of
the rest, that if the original were madder than this, it must
be incurably mad. I then translated the ode from the
Greek, and as nearly as possible, word for word; and the
impression was that in the general movement of the
periods, in the form of the connections and transitions, and
in the sober majesty of lofty sense, it appeared to them to
approach more nearly than any other poetry they had
heard to the style of our Bible in the prophetic books.
The first strophe will suffice as a specimen:

Ye harp-controlling hymns! (or) ye hymns the sovereigns
    of harps!
What God? what Hero?
What Man shall we celebrate?
Truly Pisa indeed is of Jove,
But the Olympiad (or the Olympic games) did Hercules
    establish,
The first-fruits of the spoils of war.
But Theron for the four-horsed car,
That bore victory to him,
It behooves us now to voice aloud:
The Just, the Hospitable,
The Bulwark of Agrigentum,
Of renowned fathers
The Flower, even him
Who preserves his native city erect and safe.

But are such rhetorical caprices condemnable only for
their deviation from the language of real life? and are they
by no other means to be precluded, but by the rejection of
all distinctions between prose and verse, save that of
metre? Surely good sense, and a moderate insight into
the constitution of the human mind, would be amply
sufficient to prove that such language and such combina-
tions are the native produce neither of the fancy nor of
the imagination; that their operation consists in the excite-
ment of surprise by the juxta-position and *apparent* recon-

ciliation of widely different or incompatible things. As when, for instance, the hills are made to reflect the image of a *voice*. Surely no unusual taste is requisite to see clearly that this compulsory juxta-position is not produced by the presentation of impressive or delightful forms to the inward vision, nor by any sympathy with the modifying powers with which the genius of the poet had united and inspirited all the objects of his thought; that it is therefore a species of *wit*, a pure work of the *will*, and implies a leisure and self-possession both of thought and of feeling, incompatible with the steady fervor of a mind possessed and filled with the grandeur of its subject. To sum up the whole in one sentence. When a poem, or a part of a poem, shall be adduced which is evidently vicious in the figures and contexture of its style, yet for the condemnation of which no reason can be assigned except that it differs from the style in which men actually converse, then, and not till then, can I hold this theory to be either plausible, or practicable, or capable of furnishing either rule, guidance, or precaution, that might not, more easily and more safely, as well as more naturally, have been deduced in the author's own mind from considerations of grammar, logic, and the truth and nature of things, confirmed by the authority of works, whose fame is not of ONE country, nor of ONE age.

Chapter XIX

Continuation—Concerning the real object which, it is probable, Mr. Wordsworth had before him in his critical preface—Elucidation and application of this—The neutral style, or that common to Prose and Poetry, exemplified by specimens from Chaucer, Herbert, &c.

IT MIGHT APPEAR from some passages in the former part of Mr. Wordsworth's preface that he meant to confine his theory of style, and the necessity of a close accordance with the actual language of men, to those particular subjects from low and rustic life which by way of experiment he had purposed to naturalize as a new species in our English poetry. But from the train of argument that follows; from the reference to Milton; and from the spirit of his critique on Gray's sonnet; those sentences appear to have been rather courtesies of modesty than actual limitations of his system. Yet so groundless does this system appear on a close examination, and so strange and over-whelming[1] in its consequences, that I cannot, and I do not, believe that the poet did ever himself adopt it in the unqualified sense in which his expressions have been understood by others, and which, indeed, according to all the common laws of interpretation they seem to bear. What then did he mean? I apprehend that in the clear perception, not unaccompanied with disgust or contempt, of the gaudy affectations of a style which passed too current with too many for poetic diction (though in truth it had as little pretensions to poetry as to logic or common sense), he narrowed his view for the time; and feeling a justifiable preference for the language of nature and of good sense, even in its humblest and least ornamented forms, he suffered himself to express, in terms at once too large and too exclusive, his predilection for a style the most remote possible from the false and showy splendor which he wished to explode. It is possible that this predilection, at first merely comparative, deviated for a time into direct partiality. But the real object which he had in view, was, I doubt not, a species of excellence which had been long before most happily characterized by the judicious and amiable GARVE, whose works are so justly beloved and esteemed by the Germans, in his remarks[2] on GELLERT.

However novel this phenomenon may have been in Germany at the time of Gellert, it is by no means new, nor yet of recent existence in our language. Spite of the licentiousness with which Spenser occasionally compels

---

[1] I had in my mind the striking but untranslatable epithet, which the celebrated Mendelssohn applied to the great founder of the Critical Philosophy, *"Der alleszermalmende KANT,"* i.e. the all-becrushing, or rather the *all-to-nothing-crushing* KANT. In the facility and force of compound epithets, the German from the number of its cases and inflections approaches to the Greek: that language so

"Bless'd in the happy marriage of sweet words."

It is in the woeful harshness of its sounds alone that the German need shrink from the comparison. (C.'s note)

[2] remarks here omitted. But see the ideas in C.'s next paragraph.

the orthography of his words into a subservience to his rhymes, the whole "Faery Queen" is an almost continued instance of this beauty. Waller's song "Go, lovely Rose," &c., is doubtless familiar to most of my readers; but if I had happened to have had by me the poems of COTTON, more but far less deservedly celebrated as the author of the Virgil travestied, I should have indulged myself, and I think have gratified many who are not acquainted with his serious works, by selecting some admirable specimens of this style. There are not a few poems in that volume, replete with every excellence of thought, image, and passion which we expect or desire in the poetry of the milder muse; and yet so worded that the reader sees no one reason either in the selection or the order of the words, why he might not have said the very same in an appropriate conversation, and cannot conceive how indeed he could have expressed such thoughts otherwise, without loss or injury to his meaning.[3]

Another exquisite master of this species of style, where the scholar and the poet supplies the material, but the perfect well-bred gentleman the expressions and the arrangement, is George Herbert.

Virtue

Sweet day, so cool, so calm, so bright,
The bridal of the earth and sky:
The dew shall weep thy fall to-night,
 For thou must die.

Sweet rose, whose hue angry and brave
Bids the rash gazer wipe his eye:
Thy root is ever in its grave,
 And thou must die.

Sweet spring, full of sweet days and roses,
A nest, where sweets compacted lie:
My musick shews, ye have your closes,
 And all must die.

[3] meaning C. quotes, with brief comment, a long passage from Chaucer's *Troilus and Criseyde*, short passages from Drayton's *Ideas* and Harvey's *Synagogue*, and three poems of Herbert: "Virtue," "The Bosom Sin," and "Love Unknown."

Chapter XX

The former subject continued.

I HAVE NO FEAR in declaring my conviction that the excellence defined and exemplified in the preceding chapter is not the characteristic excellence of Mr. Wordsworth's style; because I can add with equal sincerity that it is precluded by higher powers. The praise of uniform adherence to genuine, logical English is undoubtedly his; nay, laying the main emphasis on the word *uniform*, I will dare add that, of all contemporary poets, it is *his alone*. For in a less absolute sense of the word, I should certainly include MR. BOWLES, LORD BYRON, and, as to all his later writings, MR. SOUTHEY, the exceptions in their works being so few and unimportant. But of the specific excellence described in the quotation from Garve, I appear to find more and more undoubted specimens in the works of others; for instance, among the minor poems of Mr. Thomas Moore, and of our illustrious Laureate. To me it will always remain a singular and noticeable fact; that a theory which would establish this *lingua communis,* not only as the best, but as the only commendable style, should have proceeded from a poet whose diction, next to that of Shakespeare and Milton, appears to me of all others the most *individualized* and characteristic. And let it be remembered too that I am now interpreting the controverted passages of Mr. W.'s critical preface by the purpose and object which he may be supposed to have intended, rather than by the sense which the words themselves must convey, if they are taken without this allowance.

A person of any taste, who had but studied three or four of Shakespeare's principal plays, would without the name affixed scarcely fail to recognize as Shakespeare's a quotation from any other play, though but of a few lines. A similar peculiarity, though in a less degree, attends Mr. Wordsworth's style, whenever he speaks in his own person; or whenever, though under a feigned name, it is clear that he himself is still speaking, as in the different dramatis

personae of the "RECLUSE." [1] Even in the other poems,
in which he purposes to be most dramatic, there are few
in which it does not occasionally burst forth. The reader
might often address the poet in his own words with
reference to the persons introduced:

> It seems, as I retrace the ballad line by line,
> That but half of it is theirs, and the better half is thine.[2]

Who, having been previously acquainted with any con-
siderable portion of Mr. Wordsworth's publications, and
having studied them with a full feeling of the author's
genius, would not at once claim as Wordsworthian the
little poem on the rainbow?

> The child is father of the man,[3] &c.

Or in the "Lucy Gray"?

> No mate, no comrade Lucy knew;
> She dwelt on a wide moor;
> *The sweetest thing that ever grew*
> *Beside a human door.*

Or in the "Idle Shepherd-boys"?

> Along the river's stony marge
> The sand-lark chants a joyous song;
> The thrush is busy in the wood,
> And carols loud and strong.
> A thousand lambs are on the rocks,
> All newly born! both earth and sky
> Keep jubilee, and more than all,
> Those boys with their green coronal;
> They never hear the cry,
> That plaintive cry! which up the hill
> Comes from the depth of Dungeon Ghyll.

Need I mention the exquisite description of the Sea
Loch in the "Blind Highland Boy"? Who but a poet tells
a tale in such language to the little ones by the fireside
as—

[1] **Recluse** W. announced in his Preface to *The Excursion* (1814)
that it was to be the "intermediate part" of a projected poem
called *The Recluse*.
[2] **thine** "The Pet Lamb" (altered)
[3] **man** "My heart leaps up . . ."

Yet had he many a restless dream,
Both when he heard the eagle's scream,
And when he heard the torrents roar,
And heard the water beat the shore
  Near where their cottage stood.

Beside a lake their cottage stood,
Not small like ours, a peaceful flood,
But one of mighty size, and strange;
That rough or smooth, is full of change,
  And stirring in its bed.

For to this lake, by night and day,
The great sea-water finds its way
Through long, long windings of the hills,
And drinks up all the pretty rills,
  And rivers large and strong:

Then hurries back the road it came—
Returns, on errand still the same;
This did it when the earth was new;
And this for evermore will do,
  As long as earth shall last.

And with the coming of the tide,
Come boats and ships that sweetly ride,
Between the woods and lofty rocks;
And to the shepherds with their flocks
  Bring tales of distant lands.

I might quote almost the whole of his "RUTH," but take the following stanzas:

But, as you have before been told,
This stripling, sportive, gay, and bold,
And with his dancing crest,
So beautiful, through savage lands
Had roamed about with vagrant bands
  Of Indians in the West.

The wind, the tempest roaring high,
The tumult of a tropic sky,
Might well be dangerous food
For him, a youth to whom was given
So much of earth, so much of heaven,
  And such impetuous blood.

Whatever in those climes he found
Irregular in sight or sound,
Did to his mind impart

A kindred impulse, seemed allied
To his own powers, and justified
    The workings of his heart.

Nor less to feed voluptuous thought
The beauteous forms of nature wrought,
Fair trees and lovely flowers;
The breezes their own languor lent;
The stars had feelings, which they sent
    Into those magic bowers.

Yet, in his worst pursuits, I ween
That sometimes there did intervene
Pure hopes of high intent:
For passions linked to forms so fair
And stately, needs must have their share
    Of noble sentiment.

But from Mr. Wordsworth's more elevated compositions, which already form three-fourths of his works; and will, I trust, constitute hereafter a still larger proportion;—from these, whether in rhyme or blank-verse, it would be difficult and almost superfluous to select instances of a diction peculiarly his own, of a style which cannot be imitated without its being at once recognized as originating in Mr. Wordsworth. It would not be easy to open on any one of his loftier strains that does not contain examples of this; and more in proportion as the lines are more excellent, and most like the author. For those who may happen to have been less familiar with his writings, I will give three specimens taken with little choice. The first from the lines on the "BOY [4] OF WINANDERMERE," who

Blew mimic hootings to the silent owls,
That they might answer him. And they would shout
Across the watery vale, and shout again,
With long halloos, and screams, and echoes loud
Redoubled and redoubled; concourse wild
Of mirth and jocund din. And when it chanced
That pauses of deep silence mocked his skill,
Then sometimes, in that silence, while he hung
Listening, a gentle shock of mild surprise
Has carried far into his heart the voice

[4] **Boy** "There was a boy . . ."

Of mountain torrents; or the visible scene[5]
Would enter unawares into his mind
With all its solemn imagery, its rocks,
Its woods, and that uncertain heaven, received
Into the bosom of the steady lake.

The second shall be that noble imitation of Drayton[6] (if it was not rather a coincidence) in the "JOANNA."

When I had gazed perhaps two minutes' space,
Joanna, looking in my eyes, beheld
That ravishment of mine, and laughed aloud.
The rock, like something starting from a sleep,
Took up the lady's voice, and laughed again:
That ancient woman seated on HELM-CRAG
Was ready with her cavern; HAMMAR-SCAR,
And the tall steep of SILVER-HOW sent forth
A noise of laughter; southern LOUGHRIGG heard,
And FAIRFIELD answered with a mountain tone.
HELVELLYN far into the clear blue sky
Carried the lady's voice,—old SKIDDAW blew
His speaking trumpet;—back out of the clouds
From GLARAMARA southward came the voice:
And KIRKSTONE tossed it from his misty head!

The third, which is in rhyme, I take from the "Song at the feast of Brougham Castle, upon the restoration of Lord Clifford the shepherd to the estates of his ancestors."

Now another day is come,
Fitter hope, and nobler doom;
He hath thrown aside his crook,
And hath buried deep his book;
Armor rusting in the halls
On the blood of Clifford calls;
'Quell the Scot,' exclaims the lance!
'Bear me to the heart of France,'
Is the longing of the Shield—
Tell thy name, thou trembling field!
Field of death, where'er thou be,
Groan thou with our victory!
Happy day, and mighty hour,
When our shepherd, in his power,
Mailed and horsed, with lance and sword,

[5] scene C.'s long note objects to this word, except in reference to the stage
[6] **Drayton** C. quotes in a note the similar passage from the *Polyolbion*, Song XXX

To his ancestors restored,
Like a re-appearing star,
Like a glory from afar,
First shall head the flock of war!

Alas! the fervent harper did not know
That for a tranquil soul the lay was framed,
Who, long compelled in humble walks to go,
Was softened into feeling, soothed, and tamed.

Love had he found in huts where poor men lie:
His daily teachers had been woods and rills;
The silence that is in the starry sky,
The sleep that is among the lonely hills.

The words themselves, in the foregoing extracts, are,
no doubt, sufficiently common for the greater part. (But
in what poem are they not so, if we except a few mis-
adventurous attempts to translate the arts and sciences
into verse?) In the "Excursion" the number of poly-
syllabic (or what the common people call, *dictionary*)
words is more than usually great. And so must it needs be,
in proportion to the number and variety of an author's
conceptions, and his solicitude to express them with
precision. But are those words *in those places* commonly
employed in real life to express the same thought or out-
ward thing? Are they the style used in the ordinary inter-
course of spoken words? No! nor are the modes of con-
nections; and still less the breaks and transitions. Would
any but a poet—at least could any one without being
conscious that he had expressed himself with noticeable
vivacity—have described a bird singing loud by "The
thrush is *busy* in the wood"? or have spoken of boys with
a string of club-moss round their rusty hats as the boys
"*with their green coronal*"? or have translated a beautiful
May-day into "*Both earth and sky keep jubilee*"? or have
brought all the different marks and circumstances of a
sea-loch before the mind as the actions of a living and
acting power? Or have represented the reflection of the
sky in the water as "*That uncertain heaven received into
the bosom of the steady lake*"? Even the grammatical
construction is not unfrequently peculiar; as "*The wind,
the tempest roaring high, the tumult of a tropic sky,*

might well be dangerous food *to him, a youth* to whom was given, &c." There is a peculiarity in the frequent use of the ἀσυνάρτητον (i.e., the omission of the connective particle before the last of several words, or several sentences used grammatically as single words, all being in the same case and governing or governed by the same verb) and not less in the construction of words by apposition (*to him, a youth*). In short, were there excluded from Mr. Wordsworth's poetic compositions all that a literal adherence to the theory of his preface *would* exclude, two-thirds at least of the marked beauties of his poetry must be erased. For a far greater number of lines would be sacrificed than in any other recent poet; because the pleasure received from Wordsworth's poems being less derived either from excitement of curiosity or the rapid flow of narration, the *striking* passages form a larger proportion of their value. I do not adduce it as a fair criterion of comparative excellence, nor do I even think it such; but merely as matter of fact. I affirm that from no contemporary writer could so many lines be quoted, without reference to the poem in which they are found, for their own independent weight or beauty. From the sphere of my own experience I can bring to my recollection three persons of no every-day powers and acquirements, who had read the poems of others with more, and more unalloyed pleasure, and had thought more highly of their authors, as poets; who yet have confessed to me, that from no modern work had so many passages started up anew in their minds at different times, and as different occasions had awakened a meditative mood.

Chapter XXII

The characteristic defects of Wordsworth's poetry, with the principles from which the judgment, that they are defects, is deduced—Their proportion to the beauties— For the greatest part characteristic of his theory only.

If Mr. Wordsworth have set forth principles of poetry which his arguments are insufficient to support, let him and those who have adopted his sentiments be set right by the confutation of those arguments, and by the substitution of more philosophical principles. And still let the due credit be given to the portion and importance of the truths which are blended with his theory; truths the too exclusive attention to which had occasioned its errors, by tempting him to carry those truths beyond their proper limits. If his mistaken theory have at all influenced his poetic compositions, let the effects be pointed out, and the instances given. But let it likewise be shown how far the influence has acted; whether diffusively, or only by starts; whether the number and importance of the poems and passages thus infected be great or trifling compared with the sound portion; and lastly, whether they are inwoven into the texture of his works, or are loose and separable. The result of such a trial would evince beyond a doubt what it is high time to announce decisively and aloud, that the *supposed* characteristics of Mr. Wordsworth's poetry, whether admired or reprobated; whether they are simplicity or simpleness; faithful adherence to essential nature, or wilful selections from human nature of its meanest forms and under the least attractive associations; are as little the *real* characteristics of his poetry at large as of his genius and the constitution of his mind.

In a comparatively small number of poems he chose to try an experiment; and this experiment we will suppose to have failed. Yet even in these poems it is impossible not to perceive that the natural *tendency* of the poet's mind is to great objects and elevated conceptions. The poem entitled "Fidelity" is for the greater part written in language as unraised and naked as any perhaps in the two volumes. Yet take the following stanza and compare it with the preceding stanzas of the same poem.

> There sometimes does a leaping fish
> Send through the tarn a lonely cheer;
> The crags repeat the raven's croak,
> In symphony austere;
> Thither the rainbow comes—the cloud—
> And mists that spread the flying shroud;
> And sun-beams; and the sounding blast,
> That if it could would hurry past;
> But that enormous barrier binds it fast.

Or compare the four last lines of the concluding stanza with the former half.[1]

> Yes, proof was plain that since the day
> On which the traveller thus had died,
> The dog had watched about the spot,
> Or by his master's side:
> *How nourished there through such long time*
> *He knows, who gave that love sublime,*
> *And gave that strength of feeling, great*
> *Above all human estimate.*

Can any candid and intelligent mind hesitate in determining which of these best represents the tendency and native character of the poet's genius? Will he not decide that the one was written because the poet *would* so write, and the other because he could not so entirely repress the force and grandeur of his mind, but that he must in some part or other of *every* composition write otherwise? In short, that his only disease is the being out of his element; like the swan that, having amused himself for a while with crushing the weeds on the river's bank, soon returns to his own majestic movements on its reflecting and sustaining surface. Let it be observed that I am here supposing the imagined judge to whom I appeal to have already decided against the poet's theory, as far as it is different from the principles of the art, generally acknowledged.

I cannot here enter into a detailed examination of Mr. Wordsworth's works; but I will attempt to give the main results of my own judgment, after an acquaintance of many years, and repeated perusals. And though, to appreciate the defects of a great mind it is necessary to understand previously its characteristic excellences, yet I have already expressed myself with sufficient fulness to preclude most of the ill effects that might arise from my pursuing a contrary arrangement. I will, therefore, commence with what I deem the prominent *defects* of his poems hitherto published.

The first *characteristic, though only occasional* defect,

---

[1] half in the text of 1815, like all the texts of shorter poems in this chapter. W. revised most of the passages to which C. objected.

which I appear to myself to find in these poems is the IN-
CONSTANCY of the *style*. Under this name I refer to
the sudden and unprepared transitions from lines or sen-
tences of peculiar felicity (at all events striking and
original) to a style not only unimpassioned but undis-
tinguished. He sinks too often and too abruptly to that
style which I should place in the second division of
language, dividing it into the three species; *first,* that
which is peculiar to poetry; *second,* that which is only
proper in prose; and *third,* the neutral or common to both.
There have been works, such as Cowley's essay on Crom-
well, in which prose and verse are intermixed (not as in
the *Consolation* of Boetius, or the *Argenis* of Barclay, by
the insertion of poems supposed to have been spoken or
composed on occasions previously related in prose, but)
the poet passing from one to the other as the nature of
the thoughts or his own feelings dictated. Yet this mode
of composition does not satisfy a cultivated taste. There
is something unpleasant in the being thus obliged to
alternate states of feeling so dissimilar, and this too in a
species of writing, the pleasure from which is in part
derived from the preparation and previous expectation of
the reader. A portion of that awkwardness is felt which
hangs upon the introduction of songs in our modern comic
operas; and to prevent which the judicious Metastasio (as
to whose exquisite *taste* there can be no hesitation, what-
ever doubts may be entertained as to his *poetic genius*)
uniformly placed the ARIA at the end of the scene, at the
same time that he almost always raises and impassions the
style of the recitative immediately preceding. Even in real
life, the difference is great and evident between words
used as the *arbitrary marks* of thought, our smooth market-
coin of intercourse with the image and superscription worn
out by currency; and those which convey pictures either
borrowed from *one* outward object to enliven and partic-
ularize some *other;* or used allegorically to body forth the
inward state of the person speaking; or such as are at least
the exponents of his peculiar turn and unusual extent of
faculty. So much so indeed that in the social circles of
private life we often find a striking use of the latter put a
stop to the general flow of conversation, and by the ex-
citement arising from concentrated attention produce a

sort of damp and interruption for some minutes after. But
in the perusal of works of literary *art,* we *prepare* our-
selves for such language; and the business of the writer,
like that of a painter whose subject requires unusual
splendor and prominence, is so to raise the lower and
neutral tints that what in a different style would be the
commanding colors are here used as the means of that
gentle *degradation* requisite in order to produce the effect
of a *whole.* Where this is not achieved in a poem, the
metre merely reminds the reader of his claims in order to
disappoint them; and where this defect occurs frequently,
his feelings are alternately startled by anticlimax and
hyperclimax.

I refer the reader to the exquisite stanzas cited for
another purpose from "The Blind Highland Boy"; and
then annex, as being in my opinion instances of this
disharmony in style, the two following:

> And one, the rarest, was a shell,
> Which he, poor child, had studied well;
> The shell of a green turtle, thin
> And hollow;—you might sit therein,
>   It was so wide and deep.

> Our Highland Boy oft visited
> The house which held his prize; and, led
> By choice or chance, did thither come
> One day, when no one was at home,
>   And found the door unbarred.

Or page 172, vol. I.

> 'Tis gone—forgotten—*let me do*
> *My best.* There was a smile or two—
> I can remember them, I see
> The smiles worth all the world to me.
> Dear Baby, I must lay thee down:
> Thou troublest me with strange alarms;
> Smiles hast thou, sweet ones of thine own;
> I cannot keep thee in my arms;
> For they confound me: *as it is,*
> I have forgot those smiles of his! [2]

[2] his "The Emigrant Mother"

Or page 269, vol. I.

> Thou hast a nest, for thy love and thy rest,
> And though little troubled with sloth
> Drunken lark! thou would'st be loth
> To be such a traveller as I.
>   Happy, happy liver!
> *With a soul as strong as a mountain river*
> *Pouring out praise to the Almighty giver!*
> Joy and jollity be with us both!
> Hearing thee or else some other,
>   As merry a brother,
> I on the earth will go plodding on
> By myself cheerfully till the day is done.[3]

The incongruity which I appear to find in this passage is that of the two noble lines in italics with the preceding and following. See vol. II, page 30.

> Close by a pond, upon the further side,
> He stood alone; a minute's space, I guess,
> I watched him, he continuing motionless:
> To the pool's further margin then I drew,
> He being all the while before me full in view.[4]

Compare this with the repetition of the same image in the next stanza but two.

> And still as I drew near with gentle pace,
> Beside the little pond or moorish flood
> Motionless as a cloud the old man stood,
> That heareth not the loud winds as they call,
> And moveth altogether, if it move at all.

Or lastly, the second of the three following stanzas, compared both with the first and the third.

> My former thoughts returned: the fear that kills;
> And hope that is unwilling to be fed;
> Cold, pain, and labor, and all fleshly ills;
> And mighty poets in their misery dead.
> But now, perplexed by what the old man had said,
> My question eagerly did I renew,
> 'How is it that you live, and what is it you do?
>
> He with a smile did then his words repeat;
> And said, that, gathering leeches, far and wide

[3] **done** "To a Skylark"
[4] **view** "Resolution and Independence"

He travelled; stirring thus about his feet
The waters of the ponds where they abide.
'Once I could meet with them on every side,
But they have dwindled long by slow decay;
Yet still I persevere, and find them where I may.'

While he was talking thus, the lonely place,
The old man's shape, and speech, all troubled me:
In my mind's eye I seemed to see him pace
About the weary moors continually,
Wandering about alone and silently.

Indeed this fine poem is *especially* characteristic of the author. There is scarce a defect or excellence in his writings of which it would not present a specimen. But it would be unjust not to repeat that this defect is only occasional. From a careful re-perusal of the two volumes of poems, I doubt whether the objectionable passages would amount in the whole to one hundred lines; not the eighth part of the number of pages. In the "EXCURSION" the feeling of incongruity is seldom excited by the diction of any passage considered in itself, but by the sudden superiority of some other passage forming the context.

The second defect I could· generalize with tolerable accuracy, if the reader will pardon an uncouth and new-coined word. There is, I should say, not seldom a *matter-of-factness* in certain poems. This may be divided into, *first*, a laborious minuteness and fidelity in the representation of objects, and their positions, as they appeared to the poet himself; *secondly*, the insertion of accidental circumstances, in order to the full explanation of his living characters, their dispositions and actions; which circumstances might be necessary to establish the probability of a statement in real life, where nothing is taken for granted by the hearer, but appear superfluous in poetry, where the reader is willing to believe for his own sake. To this *accidentality* I object, as contravening the essence of poetry, which Aristotle pronounces to be σπουδαιότατον καὶ φιλοσοφώτατον γένος, the most intense, weighty, and philosophical product of human art; [5] adding, as the reason,

---

[5] art C. translates his own Greek, which is an adaptation of Aristotle's comparison of poetry and history (*Poetics,* IX). C. is

that it is the most catholic and abstract. The following
passage from Davenant's prefatory letter to Hobbes[6] well
expresses this truth. "When I considered the actions which
I meant to describe (those inferring the persons), I was
again persuaded rather to choose those of a former age
than the present; and in a century so far removed as might
preserve me from their improper examinations who know
not the requisites of a poem, nor how much pleasure they
lose (and even the pleasures of heroic poesy are not un-
profitable) who take away the liberty of a poet, and fetter
his feet in the shackles of an historian. For why should
a poet doubt in story to mend the intrigues of fortune by
more delightful conveyances of probable fictions, because
austere historians have entered into bond to truth? An
obligation which were in poets as foolish and unnecessary
as is the bondage of false martyrs, who lie in chains for a
mistaken opinion. *But by this I would imply, that truth
narrative and past is the idol of historians (who worship a
dead thing), and truth operative, and by effects con-
tinually alive, is the mistress of poets, who hath not her
existence in matter, but in reason.*"

For this minute accuracy in the painting of local
imagery, the lines in the EXCURSION,[7] pp. 96, 97, and
98 may be taken, if not as a striking instance, yet as an
illustration of my meaning. It must be some strong motive
(as, for instance, that the description was necessary to
the intelligibility of the tale) which could induce me to
describe in a number of verses what a draughtsman could
present to the eye with incomparably greater satisfaction
by half a dozen strokes of his pencil, or the painter with
as many touches of his brush. Such descriptions too often
occasion in the mind of a reader who is determined to

criticizing matter-of-fact naturalism by the standards of the
central classical doctrine of universal human nature in poetry,
with its corollary doctrine of appropriateness or "decorum." All
the defects of W.'s poetry which he cites are judged by these
standards, and not as failures of the romantic imagination, to
which C. might have appealed. See also the reference to
Aristotle in arguing against W.'s primitivism, (p. 40 above)
and the reference to Horace below, n. 15.

[6] **Hobbes** Preface to *Gondibert*

[7] **Excursion** III, 13-72, especially 50, etc. C. refers to the text of
1814.

understand his author, a feeling of labor, not very dissimilar to that with which he would construct a diagram, line by line, for a long geometrical proposition. It seems to be like taking the pieces of a dissected map out of its box. We first look at one part, and then at another, then join and dove-tail them; and when the successive acts of attention have been completed, there is a retrogressive effort of mind to behold it as a whole. The poet should paint to the imagination, not to the fancy; and I know no happier case to exemplify the distinction between these two faculties. Masterpieces of the former mode of poetic painting abound in the writings of Milton, *ex. gr.*,

> The fig-tree, not that kind for fruit renown'd,
> But such as at this day, to Indians known,
> In Malabar or Decan spreads her arms
> Branching so broad and long, that in the ground
> The bended twigs take root, *and daughters grow*
> *About the mother-tree, a pillar'd shade*
> *High over-arch'd, and* ECHOING WALKS BETWEEN:
> *There oft the Indian Herdsman shunning heat*
> *Shelters in cool, and tends his pasturing herds*
> *At loop holes cut through thickest shade.*
>
> MILTON, *P. L.* 9. 1101.

This is *creation* rather than *painting*, or if painting, yet such, and with such co-presence of the whole picture flashed at once upon the eye, as the sun paints in a camera obscura. But the poet must likewise understand and command what Bacon calls the *vestigia communia*[8] of the senses, the latency of all in each, and more especially as by a magical *penna duplex*,[9] the excitement of vision by sound and the exponents of sound. Thus "THE ECHOING WALKS BETWEEN" may be almost said to reverse the fable in tradition of the head of Memnon,[10] in the Egyptian statue. Such may be deservedly entitled the *creative words* in the world of imagination.

The second division respects an apparent minute adherence to *matter-of-fact* in characters and incidents; *a*

---

[8] **communia** synaesthesia. C. himself translates (freely) at once
[9] **duplex** double pen
[10] **Memnon** said to give forth a sound when struck by the light of the sun. Reversing the senses, Milton's "echoing walks" suggest by sound an image of sight.

biographical attention to probability, and an *anxiety* of explanation and retrospect. Under this head I shall deliver, with no feigned diffidence, the results of my best reflection on the great point of controversy between Mr. Wordsworth and his objectors; namely, on THE CHOICE OF HIS CHARACTERS. I have already declared and, I trust, justified, my utter dissent from the mode of argument which his critics have hitherto employed. To *their* question, Why did you choose such a character, or a character from such a rank of life? the poet might in my opinion fairly retort: why with the conception of my character did you make wilful choice of mean or ludicrous associations not furnished by me, but supplied from your own sickly and fastidious feelings? How was it, indeed, probable, that such arguments could have any weight with an author whose plan, whose guiding principle, and main object it was to attack and subdue that state of association which leads us to place the chief value on those things in which man DIFFERS from man, and to forget or disregard the high dignities which belong to HUMAN NATURE, the sense and the feeling which *may* be, and *ought* to be, found in *all* ranks? The feelings with which, as Christians, we contemplate a mixed congregation rising or kneeling before their common Maker, Mr. Wordsworth would have us entertain at *all* times, as men and as readers; and by the excitement of this lofty, yet prideless impartiality in *poetry,* he might hope to have encouraged its continuance in *real life.* The praise of good men be his! In real life, and, I trust, even in my imagination, I honor a virtuous and wise man, without reference to the presence or absence of artificial advantages. Whether in the person of an armed baron, a laureled bard, &c., or of an old pedlar, or still older leech-gatherer, the same qualities of head and heart must claim the same reverence. And even in poetry I am not conscious that I have ever suffered my feelings to be disturbed or offended by any thoughts or images which the poet himself has not presented.

But yet I object, nevertheless, and for the following reasons. First, because the object in view, as an *immediate* object, belongs to the moral philosopher, and would be pursued, not only more appropriately, but in my opinion with far greater probability of success, in sermons or moral essays than in an elevated poem. It seems, indeed, to destroy the main fundamental distinction, not only between a *poem* and *prose,* but even between philosophy and works of fiction, inasmuch as it proposes *truth* for its immediate object instead of *pleasure.* Now till the blessed time shall come when truth itself shall be pleasure, and both shall be so united as to be distinguishable in words only, not in feeling, it will remain the poet's office to proceed upon that state of association, which actually exists as *general;* instead of attempting first to *make* it what it ought to be, and then to let the pleasure follow. But here is unfortunately a small *hysteron-proteron.*[11] For the communication of pleasure is the introductory means by which alone the poet must expect to moralize his readers. Secondly: though I were to admit, for a moment, *this* argument to be groundless: yet how is the moral effect to be produced by merely attaching the name of some low profession to powers which are *least* likely, and to qualities which are assuredly not *more* likely, to be found in it? The poet, speaking in his own person, may at once delight and improve us by sentiments which teach us the independence of goodness, of wisdom, and even of genius, on the favors of fortune. And having made a due reverence before the throne of Antonine, he may bow with equal awe before Epictetus among his fellow-slaves—

> and rejoice
> In the plain presence of his dignity.[12]

Who is not at once delighted and improved, when the POET Wordsworth himself exclaims,

> O many are the poets that are sown
> By Nature; men endowed with highest gifts,
> The vision and the faculty divine,
> Yet wanting the accomplishment of verse,
> Nor having e'er, as life advanced, been led
> By circumstance to take unto the height
> The measure of themselves, these favored beings,
> All but a scattered few, live out their time

[11] hysteron-proteron latter-former, the cart before the horse
[12] dignity *Excursion,* I, 75-76

Husbanding that which they possess within,
And go to the grave unthought of. Strongest minds
Are often those of whom the noisy world
Hears least.

EXCURSION,[13] B. I.

To use a colloquial phrase, such sentiments, in such language, do one's heart good; though I for my part, have not the fullest faith in the *truth* of the observation. On the contrary I believe the instances to be exceedingly rare; and should feel almost as strong an objection to introduce such a character in a poetic fiction as a pair of black swans on a lake in a fancy-landscape. When I think how many, and how much better books than Homer, or even than Herodotus, Pindar, or Aeschylus, could have read, are in the power of almost every man, in a country where almost every man is instructed to read and write; and how restless, how difficultly hidden, the powers of genius are; and yet find even in situations the most favorable, according to Mr. Wordsworth, for the formation of a pure and poetic language; in situations which ensure familiarity with the grandest objects of the imagination; but *one* BURNS, among the shepherds of *Scotland,* and not a single poet of humble life among those of *English* lakes and mountains; I conclude that POETIC GENIUS is not only a very delicate but a very rare plant.

But be this as it may, the feelings with which

I think of CHATTERTON, the marvellous boy,
The sleepless soul that perished in his pride;
Of BURNS, that walked in glory and in joy
Behind his plough upon the mountain-side—[14]

are widely different from those with which I should read a *poem* where the author, having occasion for the character of a poet and a philosopher in the fable of his narration, had chosen to make him a *chimney-sweeper;* and then, in order to remove all doubts on the subject, had *invented* an account of his birth, parentage and education, with all the strange and fortunate accidents which had concurred in making him at once poet, philosopher, and sweep! Nothing but biography can justify this. If it

[13] **Excursion** I, 77-93, with five lines omitted
[14] **side** "Resolution and Independence"

be admissible even in a *novel,* it must be one in the manner of De Foe's, that were meant to pass for histories, not in the manner of Fielding's: in the life of Moll Flanders or Colonel Jack, not in a Tom Jones or even a Joseph Andrews. Much less then can it be legitimately introduced in a *poem,* the characters of which, amid the strongest individualization, must still remain representative. The precepts of Horace[15] on this point, are grounded on the nature both of poetry and of the human mind. They are not more peremptory than wise and prudent. For in the first place a deviation from them perplexes the reader's feelings, and all the circumstances which are feigned in order to make such accidents less improbable, divide and disquiet his faith, rather than aid and support it. Spite of all attempts, the fiction *will* appear, and unfortunately not as *fictitious* but as *false.* The reader not only *knows* that the sentiments and language are the poet's own, and his own too in his *artificial* character, as *poet;* but by the fruitless endeavors to make him think the contrary, he is not even suffered to *forget* it. The effect is similar to that produced by an epic poet when the fable and the characters are *derived* from Scripture history, as in the *Messiah* of Klopstock, or in Cumberland's *Calvary:*[16] and not merely *suggested* by it, as in the *Paradise Lost* of Milton. That *illusion,*[17] contradistinguished from *delusion,* that *negative* faith, which simply permits the images presented to work by their own force, without either denial or affirmation of their real existence by the judgment, is rendered impossible by their immediate neighborhood to words and facts of known and absolute truth. A faith which transcends even historic belief must absolutely *put out* this mere poetic analogon of faith, as the summer sun is said to extinguish our household fires when it shines full upon them. What would otherwise have been yielded to as pleasing fiction is repelled as revolting falsehood. The effect produced in this latter case by the solemn belief of the reader is in a less degree brought about in the instances to which I have been objecting by the baffled attempts of the author to *make* him believe.

[15] **Horace** an invocation of the classical doctrine of decorum
[16] **Calvary** a blank verse epic of 1792
[17] **illusion** cf. p. 29, n. 1 above

Add to all the foregoing the seeming uselessness both
of the project and of the anecdotes from which it is to
derive support. Is there one word, for instance, attributed
to the pedlar in the "EXCURSION," characteristic of a
pedlar? One sentiment that might not more plausibly, even
without the aid of any previous explanation, have pro-
ceeded from any wise and beneficent old man, of a rank
or profession in which the language of learning and refine-
ment are natural and to be expected? Need the rank
have been at all particularized where nothing follows
which the knowledge of that rank is to explain or illus-
trate? When on the contrary this information renders the
man's language, feelings, sentiments, and information a
riddle which must itself be solved by episodes of anecdote?
Finally when this, and this alone, could have induced a
genuine *poet* to inweave in a poem of the loftiest style,
and on subjects the loftiest and of most universal interest,
such minute matters of fact (not unlike those furnished
for the obituary of a magazine by the friends of some
obscure *ornament of society lately deceased* in some
obscure town) as

> Among the hills of Athol he was born:
> There, on a small hereditary farm,
> An unproductive slip of rugged ground,
> His father dwelt; and died in poverty;
> While he, whose lowly fortune I retrace,
> The youngest of three sons, was yet a babe,
> A little one—unconscious of their loss.
> But, ere he had outgrown his infant days,
> His widowed mother, for a second mate,
> Espoused the teacher of the village school;
> Who on her offspring zealously bestowed
> Needful instruction.
>
> From his sixth year, the boy of whom I speak,
> In summer tended cattle on the hills;
> But, through the inclement and the perilous days
> Of long-continuing winter, he repaired
> To his step-father's school.[18]

For all the admirable passages interposed in this narra-

[18] **school** *Excursion,* I, 108-122. C. quotes the 1814 text, from
which W. eliminated the minute matters of fact.

tion might, with trifling alterations, have been far more appropriately, and with far greater verisimilitude, told of a poet in the character of a poet; and without incurring another defect which I shall now mention, and a sufficient illustration of which will have been here anticipated.

Third: an undue predilection for the *dramatic* form in certain poems, from which one or other of two evils result. Either the thoughts and diction are different from that of the poet, and then there arises an incongruity of style; or they are the same and indistinguishable, and then it presents a species of ventriloquism, where two are represented as talking, while in truth one man only speaks.

The fourth class of defects is closely connected with the former; but yet are such as arise likewise from an intensity of feeling disproportionate to *such* knowledge and value of the objects described as can be fairly antici-pated of men in general, even of the most cultivated classes; and with which therefore few only, and those few particularly circumstanced, can be supposed to sympathize. In this class I comprize occasional prolixity, repetition, and an eddying instead of progression of thought. As instances, see pages 27, 28, and 62 of the *Poems*, Vol. I,[19] and the first eighty lines of the Sixth Book of the *Excursion*.

Fifth and last; thoughts and images too great for the subject. This is an approximation to what might be called *mental* bombast, as distinguished from verbal: for, as in the latter there is a disproportion of the expressions to the thoughts, so in this there is a disproportion of thought to the circumstance and occasion. This, by the bye, is a fault of which none but a man of genius is capable. It is the awkwardness and strength of Hercules with the distaff of Omphale.

It is a well-known fact that bright colors in motion both make and leave the strongest impressions on the eye. Nothing is more likely too than that a vivid image or visual spectrum, thus originated, may become the link of association in recalling the feelings and images that had

[19] vol. I "Anecdote for Fathers" (pp. 27, 28) and possibly "Song at the Feast of Brougham Castle," 11. 87-101 (vol. II, p. 62). This is Sara Coleridge's suggestion for vol. I, p. 62, since that page is blank.

accompanied the original impression. But if we describe
this in such lines as

> They flash upon that inward eye,
> Which is the bliss of solitude,[20]

in what words shall we describe the joy of retrospection,
when the images and virtuous actions of a whole well-
spent life pass before that conscience which is indeed the
inward eye: which is indeed *"the bliss of solitude"*?
Assuredly we seem to sink most abruptly, not to say
burlesquely, and almost as in a *medley*, from this couplet
to—

> And then my heart with pleasure fills,
> And dances with the *daffodils*.

> Vol. I, p. 320.

The second instance is from Vol. II, page 12, where
the poet, having gone out for a day's tour of pleasure,
meets early in the morning with a knot of *gypsies*, who
had pitched their blanket-tents and straw-beds, together
with their children and asses, in some field by the road-
side. At the close of the day on his return our tourist
found them in the same place. "Twelve hours," says he,

> Twelve hours, twelve bounteous hours, are gone, while I
> Have been a traveller under open sky,
> Much witnessing of change and cheer,
> Yet as I left I find them here! [21]

Whereat the poet, without seeming to reflect that the
poor tawny wanderers might probably have been tramping
for weeks together through road and lane, over moor and
mountain, and consequently must have been right glad
to rest themselves, their children and cattle, for one whole
day; and overlooking the obvious truth that such repose
might be quite as necessary for *them* as a walk of the
same continuance was pleasing or healthful for the more
fortunate poet; expresses his indignation in a series of lines,
the diction and imagery of which would have been rather
above than below the mark, had they been applied to the
immense empire of China improgressive for thirty cen-
turies:

[20] solitude "I wandered lonely as a cloud"
[21] here "Gipsies"

The weary SUN betook himself to rest.
—Then issued VESPER from the fulgent west,
Outshining, like a visible God,
The glorious path in which he trod!
And now, ascending, after one dark hour,
And one night's diminution of her power,
Behold the mighty MOON! this way
She looks, as if at them—but they
Regard not her:—oh, better wrong and strife,
Better vain deeds or evil than such life!
The silent HEAVENS have goings on:
The STARS have tasks!—but *these* have none!

The last instance of this defect (for I know no other than these already cited) is from the Ode,[22] page 351, Vol. II, where, speaking of a child, "a six years' darling of a pigmy size," he thus addresses him:

Thou best philosopher, who yet dost keep
Thy heritage! Thou eye among the blind,
That, deaf and silent, read'st the eternal deep,
Haunted for ever by the Eternal Mind,—
Mighty Prophet! Seer blest!
On whom those truths do rest,
Which we are toiling all our lives to find!
Thou, over whom thy immortality
Broods like the day, a master o'er a slave,
A presence that is not to be put by!

Now here, not to stop at the daring spirit of metaphor which connects the epithets "deaf and silent" with the apostrophized *eye:* or (if we are to refer it to the preceding word, philosopher) the faulty and equivocal syntax of the passage; and without examining the propriety of making a "master *brood* o'er a slave," or the *day* brood *at all;* we will merely ask, what does all this mean? In what sense is a child of that age a *philosopher?* In what sense does he *read* "the eternal deep"? In what sense is he declared to be *"for ever haunted"* by the Supreme Being? or so inspired as to deserve the splendid titles of a *mighty prophet,* a *blessed seer?* By reflection? by knowledge? by conscious intuition? or by *any* form or modification of consciousness? These would be tidings indeed; but such as would presuppose an immediate revelation to the

[22] **Ode** "Intimations of Immortality"

inspired communicator, and require miracles to authenticate his inspiration. Children at this age give us no such information of themselves; and at what time were we dipped in the Lethe which has produced such utter oblivion of a state so godlike? There are many of us that still possess some remembrances, more or less distinct, respecting themselves at six years old; pity that the worthless straws only should float, while treasures, compared with which all the mines of Golconda and Mexico were but straws, should be absorbed by some unknown gulf into some unknown abyss.

But if this be too wild and exorbitant to be suspected as having been the poet's meaning; if these mysterious gifts, faculties, and operations, are *not* accompanied with consciousness; who *else* is conscious of them? or how can it be called the child, if it be no part of the child's conscious being? For aught I know, the thinking Spirit within me may be *substantially* one with the principle of life and of vital operation. For aught I know, it may be employed as a secondary agent in the marvellous organization and organic movements of my body. But, surely, it would be strange language to say, that *I* construct my *heart!* or that *I* propel the finer influences through my *nerves!* or that *I* compress my brain, and draw the curtains of sleep round my own eyes! SPINOZA and BEHMEN were, on different systems, both Pantheists; and among the ancients there were philosophers, teachers of the EN KAI ΠAN,[23] who not only taught that God was All, but that this All constituted God. Yet not even these would confound the *part, as* a part,[24] with the Whole, *as* the whole. Nay, in no system is the distinction between the individual and God, between the Modification, and the one only Substance, more sharply drawn, than in that of SPINOZA. JACOBI indeed relates of LESSING that, after a conversation with him at the house of the poet, GLEIM (the Tyrtaeus and Anacreon of the German Parnassus) in which conversation L. had avowed privately to Jacobi his reluctance to admit any *personal* existence of the Supreme Being, or the *possibility* of personality except in a finite Intellect,

[23] EN KAI ΠAN one and all
[24] part the finite individual consciousness with the consciousness of God, of which it is a part

and while they were sitting at table, a shower of rain came
on unexpectedly. Gleim expressed his regret at the cir-
cumstance, because they had meant to drink their wine in
the garden: upon which Lessing in one of his half-earnest
half-joking moods, nodded to Jacobi, and said, "It is *I,*
perhaps, that am doing *that,*" i.e., *raining!* and J. answered,
"or perhaps I"; Gleim contented himself with staring at
them both, without asking for any explanation.

So with regard to this passage. In what sense can the
magnificent attributes above quoted be appropriated to a
child, which would not make them equally suitable to a
bee, or a *dog,* or a *field of corn;* or even to a ship, or to
the wind and waves that propel it? The omnipresent Spirit
works equally in them as in the child; and the child is
equally unconscious of it as they. It cannot surely be that
the four lines immediately following are to contain the
explanation?

> To whom the grave
> Is but a lonely bed without the sense or sight
> Of day or the warm light,
> A place of thought where we in waiting lie.

Surely, it cannot be that this wonder-rousing apostrophe
is but a comment on the little poem of "We are seven"?
that the whole meaning of the passage is reducible to the
assertion that a *child,* who by the bye at six years old
would have been better instructed [25] in most Christian
families, has no other notion of death than that of lying
in a dark, cold place? And still, I hope, not as in a *place
of thought!* not the frightful notion of lying *awake* in his
grave! The analogy between death and sleep is too simple,
too natural, to render so horrid a belief possible for chil-
dren; even had they not been in the habit, as all Christian
children are, of hearing the latter term used to express the
former. But if the child's belief be only that "he is not
dead, but sleepeth:" wherein does it differ from that of
his father and mother, or any other adult and instructed
person? To form an idea of a thing's becoming nothing,
or of nothing becoming a thing, is impossible to all finite
beings alike, of whatever age, and however educated

[25] **instructed** C. takes these lines (later omitted) to imply the
resurrection of the flesh

or uneducated. Thus it is with splendid paradoxes in general. If the words are taken in the common sense, they convey an absurdity; and if, in contempt of dictionaries and custom, they are so interpreted as to avoid the absurdity, the meaning dwindles into some bald truism. Thus you must at once understand the words *contrary* to their common import in order to arrive at any *sense;* and *according* to their common import, if you are to receive from them any feeling of *sublimity* or *admiration.*

Though the instances of this defect in Mr. Wordsworth's poems are so few that for themselves it would have been scarcely just to attract the reader's attention toward them; yet I have dwelt on it, and perhaps the more for this very reason. For being so very few, they cannot sensibly detract from the reputation of an author, who is even characterized by the number of profound truths in his writings which will stand the severest analysis; and yet few as they are, they are exactly those passages which his *blind* admirers would be most likely, and best able, to imitate. But WORDSWORTH, where he is indeed Wordsworth, may be mimicked by copyists, he may be plundered by Plagiarists; but he can not be imitated, except by those who are not born to be imitators. For without his depth of feeling and his imaginative power his *sense* would want its vital warmth and peculiarity; and without his strong sense, his *mysticism* would become *sickly*—mere fog, and dimness!

To these defects which, as appears by the extracts, are only occasional, I may oppose, with far less fear of encountering the dissent of any candid and intelligent reader, the following (for the most part correspondent) excellences. First, an austere purity of language both grammatically and logically; in short a perfect appropriateness of the words to the meaning. Of how high value I deem this, and how particularly estimable I hold the example at the present day, has been already stated: and in part too the reasons on which I ground both the moral and intellectual importance of habituating ourselves to a strict accuracy of expression. It is noticeable how limited an acquaintance with the masterpieces of art will suffice to form a correct and even a sensitive taste, where none but masterpieces have been seen and admired: while on the other hand, the most correct notions, and the widest

acquaintance with the works of excellence of all ages and
countries, will not perfectly secure us against the con-
tagious familiarity with the far more numerous offspring
of tastelessness or of a perverted taste. If this be the
case, as it notoriously is, with the arts of music and paint-
ing, much more difficult will it be to avoid the infection
of multiplied and daily examples in the practice of an
art which uses words, and words only, as its instruments.
In poetry, in which every line, every phrase, may pass
the ordeal of deliberation and deliberate choice, it is
possible, and barely possible, to attain that ultimatum
which I have ventured to propose as the infallible test of a
blameless style; namely, its *untranslatableness* in words
of the same language without injury to the meaning. Be it
observed, however, that I include in the *meaning* of a
word not only its correspondent object, but likewise all the
associations which it recalls. For language is framed to
convey not the object alone, but likewise the character,
mood, and intentions of the person who is representing it.
In poetry it *is* practicable to preserve the diction uncor-
rupted by the affectations and misappropriations which
promiscuous authorship, and reading not promiscuous only
because it is disproportionately most conversant with the
compositions of the day, have rendered general. Yet even
to the poet, composing in his own province, it is an ardu-
ous work: and as the result and pledge of a watchful
good sense, of fine and luminous distinction, and of com-
plete self-possession, may justly claim all the honor which
belongs to an attainment equally difficult and valuable,
and the more valuable for being rare. It is at *all* times the
proper food of the understanding; but in an age of corrupt
eloquence it is both food and antidote.

In prose I doubt whether it be even possible to preserve
our style wholly unalloyed by the vicious phraseology
which meets us everywhere, from the sermon to the news-
paper, from the harangue of the legislator to the speech
from the convivial chair, announcing a *toast* or senti-
ment. Our chains rattle, even while we are complaining of
them. The poems of Boetius rise high in our estimation
when we compare them with those of his contemporaries,
as Sidonius Apollinaris, &c. They might even be referred
to a purer age but that the prose in which they are set,

as jewels in a crown of lead or iron, betrays the true age of
the writer. Much, however, may be effected by education.
I believe not only from grounds of reason, but from having
in great measure assured myself of the fact by actual
though limited experience, that to a youth led from his
first boyhood to investigate the meaning of every word and
the reason of its choice and position, Logic presents itself
as an old acquaintance under new names.

On some future occasion, more especially demanding
such disquisition, I shall attempt to prove the close con-
nection between veracity and habits of mental accuracy;
the beneficial after-effects of verbal precision in the pre-
clusion of fanaticism, which masters the feelings more
especially by indistinct watch-words; and to display the
advantages which language alone, at least which language
with incomparably greater ease and certainty than any
other means, presents to the instructor of impressing modes
of intellectual energy so constantly, so imperceptibly, and
as it were by such elements and atoms, as to secure in
due time the formation of a second nature. When we
reflect that the cultivation of the judgment is a positive
command of the moral law, since the reason can give the
principle alone, and the conscience bears witness only to
the *motive*, while the application and effects must depend
on the judgment: when we consider that the greater part
of our success and comfort in life depends on distinguish-
ing the similar from the same, that which is peculiar in
each thing from that which it has in common with others,
so as still to select the most probable, instead of the
merely possible or positively unfit, we shall learn to value
earnestly and with a practical seriousness a mean, already
prepared for us by nature and society, of teaching the
young mind to think well and wisely by the same unremem-
bered process and with the same never forgotten results
as those by which it is taught to speak and converse. Now
how much warmer the interest is, how much more genial
the feelings of reality and practicability, and thence how
much stronger the impulses to imitation are which a
contemporary writer, and especially a contemporary *poet*,
excites in youth and commencing manhood, has been
treated of in the earlier pages of these sketches. I have
only to add that all the praise which is due to the exertion

of such influence for a purpose so important, joined with that which must be claimed for the infrequency of the same excellence in the same perfection, belongs in full right to Mr. WORDSWORTH. I am far, however, from denying that we have poets whose *general* style possesses the same excellence, as Mr. Moore, Lord Byron, Mr. Bowles, and, in all his later and more important works, our laurel-honoring Laureate. But there are none in whose works I do not appear to myself to find *more* exceptions than in those of Wordsworth. Quotations or specimens would here be wholly out of place, and must be left for the critic who doubts and would invalidate the justice of this eulogy so applied.

The second characteristic excellence of Mr. W.'s works is a correspondent weight and sanity of the thoughts and sentiments—won, not from books, but—from the poet's own meditative observation. They are *fresh* and have the dew upon them. His muse, at least when in her strength of wing, and when she hovers aloft in her proper element,

> Makes audible a linked lay of truth,
> Of truth profound a sweet continuous lay,
> Not learnt, but native, her own natural notes!
>
> S. T. C.[26]

Even throughout his smaller poems there is scarcely one which is not rendered valuable by some just and original reflection.

See page 25, vol. 2nd:[27] or the two following passages in one of his humblest compositions.[28]

> O Reader! had you in your mind
> Such stores as silent thought can bring,
> O gentle Reader! you would find
> A tale in every thing;

and

> I've heard of hearts unkind, kind deeds
> With coldness still returning.
> Alas! the gratitude of men
> Has oftener left me mourning;

[26] S.T.C. "To William Wordsworth"
[27] vol. 2nd "Star -Gazers"
[28] compositions "Simon Lee"

or in a still higher strain the six beautiful quatrains,[29]
page 134.

> Thus fares it still in our decay:
> And yet the wiser mind
> Mourns less for what age takes away
> Than what it leaves behind.
>
> The blackbird in the summer trees,
> The lark upon the hill,
> Let loose their carols when they please,
> Are quiet when they will.
>
> With nature never do *they* wage
> A foolish strife; they see
> A happy youth, and their old age
> Is beautiful and free!
>
> But we are pressed by heavy laws;
> And often, glad no more,
> We wear a face of joy, because
> We have been glad of yore.
>
> If there is one who need bemoan
> His kindred laid in earth,
> The household hearts that were his own,
> It is the man of mirth.
>
> My days, my friend, are almost gone,
> My life has been approved,
> And many love me; but by none
> Am I enough beloved.

or the sonnet on Buonaparte,[30] page 202, vol. 2; or finally
(for a volume would scarce suffice to exhaust the in-
stances), the last stanza of the poem on the withered
Celandine,[31] vol. 2, p. 312.

> To be a prodigal's favorite—then, worse truth,
> A miser's pensioner—behold our lot!
> O man! that from thy fair and shining youth
> Age might but take the things youth needed not.

Both in respect of this and of the former excellence,
Mr. Wordsworth strikingly resembles Samuel Daniel, one

---

[29] quatrains "The Fountain"
[30] Buonaparte "I grieved for Buonaparte"
[31] Celandine "The Small Celandine"

of the golden writers of our golden Elizabethan age, now most causelessly neglected: Samuel Daniel, whose diction bears no mark of time, no distinction of age, which has been, and as long as our language shall last, will be so far the language of the to-day and for ever, as that it is more intelligible to us than the transitory fashions of our own particular age. A similar praise is due to his sentiments. No frequency of perusal can deprive them of their freshness. For though they are brought into the full daylight of every reader's comprehension; yet are they drawn up from depths which few in any age are privileged to visit, into which few in any age have courage or inclination to descend. If Mr. Wordsworth is not equally with Daniel alike intelligible to all readers of average understanding in all passages of his works, the comparative difficulty does not arise from the greater impurity of the ore but from the nature and uses of the metal. A poem is not necessarily obscure because it does not aim to be popular. It is enough if a work be perspicuous to those for whom it is written, and

Fit audience find, though few.[32]

To the "Ode on the intimations of immortality from recollections of early childhood" the poet might have prefixed the lines which Dante addresses to one of his own Canzoni—

Canzon, io credo, che saranno radi
Che tua ragione intendan bene,
Tanto lor sei faticoso ed alto.

O lyric song, there will be few, think I,
Who may thy import understand aright:
Thou art for *them* so arduous and so high! [33]

But the ode was intended for such readers only as had been accustomed to watch the flux and reflux of their inmost nature, to venture at times into the twilight realms of consciousness, and to feel a deep interest in modes of inmost being, to which they know that the attributes of time and space are inapplicable and alien, but which yet

[32] few *Paradise Lost,* vii, 31
[33] high *Convivio,* II, Canzone I

can not be conveyed, save in symbols of time and space. For such readers the sense is sufficiently plain, and they will be as little disposed to charge Mr. Wordsworth with believing the Platonic pre-existence in the ordinary interpretation of the words as I am to believe that Plato himself ever meant or taught it.

> Πολλά μοι ὑπ᾽ ἀγκῶ-
> νος ὠκέα βέλη
> ἔνδον ἐντὶ φαρέτρας
> φωνᾶντα συνετοῖσιν ἐς
> δὲ τὸ πᾶν ἑρμηνέων
> χατίζει. σοφὸς ὁ πολ-
> λὰ εἰδὼς φυᾷ.
> μαθόντες δέ, λάβροι
> παγγλωσσίᾳ, κόρακες ὥς,
> ἄκραντα γαρύετον
> Διὸς πρὸς ὄρνιχα θεῖον.[34]

Third (and wherein he soars far above Daniel) the sinewy strength and originality of single lines and paragraphs: the frequent *curiosa felicitas* of his diction, of which I need not here give specimens, having anticipated them in a preceding page. This beauty, and as eminently characteristic of Wordsworth's poetry, his rudest assailants have felt themselves compelled to acknowledge and admire.

Fourth: the perfect truth of nature in his images and descriptions, as taken immediately from nature, and proving a long and genial intimacy with the very spirit which gives the physiognomic expression to all the works of nature. Like a green field reflected in a calm and perfectly transparent lake, the image is distinguished from the reality only by its greater softness and lustre. Like the moisture or the polish on a pebble, genius neither distorts nor false-colors its objects; but on the contrary brings out

[34] θεῖον Pindar, Olympiad II, Sandys translation, Loeb Classical Library: "Full many a swift arrow have I beneath mine arm, within my quiver, many an arrow that is vocal to the wise: but for the crowd they need interpreters. The true poet is he who knoweth much by gift of nature, but they that have only learnt the lore of song, and are turbulent and intemperate of tongue, like a pair of crows, chatter in vain against the god-like bird of Zeus."

many a vein and many a tint which escape the eye of common observation, thus raising to the rank of gems what had been often kicked away by the hurrying foot of the traveller on the dusty high road of custom.

Let me refer to the whole description of skating, vol. I, page 44 to 47, especially to the lines

> So through the darkness and the cold we flew,
> And not a voice was idle: with the din
> Meanwhile the precipices rang aloud;
> The leafless trees and every icy crag
> Tinkled like iron; while the distant hills
> Into the tumult sent an alien sound
> Of melancholy, not unnoticed, while the stars
> Eastward were sparkling clear, and in the west
> The orange sky of evening died away.[35]

Or to the poem on the green linnet, vol. I, page 244. What can be more accurate yet more lovely than the two concluding stanzas?

> Upon yon tuft of hazel trees,
> That twinkle to the gusty breeze,
> Behold him perched in ecstasies,
>   Yet seeming still to hover;
> There! where the flutter of his wings
> Upon his back and body flings
> Shadows and sunny glimmerings,
>   That cover him all over.
>
> While thus before my eyes he gleams,
> A brother of the leaves he seems;
> When in a moment forth he teems
>   His little song in gushes:
> As if it pleased him to disdain
> And mock the form which he did feign,
> While he was dancing with the train
>   Of leaves among the bushes.

Or the description of the blue-cap, and of the noontide silence,[36] page 284; or the poem to the cuckoo, page 299; or, lastly, though I might multiply the references to ten times the number, to the poem, so completely Wordsworth's, commencing

[35] away "Influence of Natural Objects"
[36] silence "The Kitten and the Falling Leaves"

"Three years she grew in sun and shower," &c.

Fifth: a meditative pathos, a union of deep and subtle thought with sensibility; a sympathy with man as man; the sympathy indeed of a contemplator, rather than a fellow-sufferer or co-mate (*spectator, haud particeps*) but of a contemplator from whose view no difference of rank conceals the sameness of the nature; no injuries of wind or weather, of toil, or even of ignorance, wholly disguise the human face divine. The superscription and the image of the Creator still remain legible to *him* under the dark lines with which guilt or calamity had cancelled or cross-barred it. Here the man and the poet lose and find themselves in each other, the one as glorified, the latter as substantiated. In this mild and philosophic pathos Wordsworth appears to me without a compeer. Such he *is:* so he *writes.* See vol. I, page 134 to 136,[37] or that most affecting composition, the "Affliction of Margaret ———— of ————," page 165 to 168, which no mother and, if I may judge by my own experience, no parent can read without a tear. Or turn to that genuine lyric, in the former edition[38] entitled "The Mad Mother," page 174 to 178, of which I cannot refrain from quoting two of the stanzas, both of them for their pathos, and the former for the fine transition in the two concluding lines of the stanza, so expressive of that deranged state in which from the increased sensibility the sufferer's attention is abruptly drawn off by every trifle, and in the same instant plucked back again by the one despotic thought, and bringing home with it, by the blending, *fusing* power of imagination and passion, the alien object to which it had been so abruptly diverted, no longer an alien but an ally and an inmate.

> Suck, little babe, oh suck again!
> It cools my blood; it cools my brain:
> Thy lips, I feel them, baby! they
> Draw from my heart the pain away.
> Oh! press me with thy little hand;
> It loosens something at my chest:

[37] **136** "Tis said that some have died for love"
[38] **edition** *Lyrical Ballads.* "The Mad Mother" is now called "Her eyes are wild."

About that tight and deadly band
I feel thy little fingers prest.
The breeze I see is in the tree!
It comes to cool my babe and me.

Thy father cares not for my breast,
'Tis thine, sweet baby, there to rest,
'Tis all thine own!—and, if its hue
Be changed, that was so fair to view,
'Tis fair enough for thee, my dove!
My beauty, little child, is flown,
But thou wilt live with me in love;
And what if my poor cheek be brown?
'Tis well for me, thou canst not see
How pale and wan it else would be.

Last, and pre-eminently, I challenge for this poet the
gift of IMAGINATION in the highest and strictest sense
of the word. In the play of *Fancy*, Wordsworth, to my
feelings, is not always graceful, and sometimes *recondite*.
The *likeness* is occasionally too strange, or demands too
peculiar a point of view, or is such as appears the creature
of predetermined research rather than spontaneous presen-
tation. Indeed his fancy seldom displays itself as mere and
unmodified fancy. But in imaginative power he stands
nearest of all modern writers to Shakespeare and Milton;
and yet in a kind perfectly unborrowed and his own. To
employ his own words, which are at once an instance
and an illustration, he does indeed to all thoughts and to
all objects

> add the gleam,
> The light that never was, on sea or land,
> The consecration, and the poet's dream.[39]

I shall select a few examples as most obviously mani-
festing this faculty; but if I should ever be fortunate
enough to render my analysis of imagination, its origin
and characters, thoroughly intelligible to the reader, he will
scarcely open on a page of this poet's works without
recognizing, more or less, the presence and the influences
of this faculty.

From the poem on the "Yew Trees," vol. I, page 303,
304.

[39] **dream** "Elegiac Stanzas"

But worthier still of note
Are those fraternal four of Borrowdale,
Joined in one solemn and capacious grove:
Huge trunks!—and each particular trunk a growth
Of intertwisted fibres serpentine
Up-coiling, and inveterately convolved,—
Nor uninformed with phantasy, and looks
That threaten the profane;—a pillared shade,
Upon whose grassless floor of red-brown hue,
By sheddings from the pining umbrage tinged
Perennially—beneath whose sable roof
Of boughs, as if for festal purpose decked
With unrejoicing berries, ghostly shapes
May meet at noontide—FEAR and trembling HOPE,
SILENCE and FORESIGHT—DEATH, the skeleton,
And TIME, the shadow—there to celebrate,
As in a natural temple scattered o'er
With altars undisturbed of mossy stone,
United worship; or in mute repose
To lie, and listen to the mountain flood
Murmuring from Glaramara's inmost caves.

The effect of the old man's figure in the poem of "Resignation[40] and Independence," vol. II, page 33.

While he was talking thus, the lonely place,
The old man's shape, and speech, all troubled me:
In my mind's eye I seemed to see him pace
About the weary moors continually,
Wandering about alone and silently.

Or the 8th, 9th, 19th, 26th, 31st, and 33d, in the collection of miscellaneous sonnets—the sonnet on the subjugation of Switzerland, page 210,[41] or the last ode, from which I especially select the two following stanzas or paragraphs, page 349 to 350.

Our birth is but a sleep and a forgetting;
The soul that rises with us, our life's star,
Hath had elsewhere its setting,
And cometh from afar.
Not in entire forgetfulness,

[40] Resignation "Resolution and Independence"
[41] 210 These sonnets begin as follows: "Where lies the land," "Even as a dragon's eye," "O mountain stream," "Earth has not anything to show," "Methought I saw," "It is a beauteous evening," "Two voices are there."

And not in utter nakedness,
But trailing clouds of glory do we come
From God, who is our home:
Heaven lies about us in our infancy!
Shades of the prison-house begin to close
    Upon the growing boy;
But he beholds the light, and whence it flows,
    He sees it in his joy!
The youth who daily further from the east
Must travel, still is nature's priest,
    And by the vision splendid
    Is on his way attended;
At length the man perceives it die away,
And fade into the light of common day.

And page 352 to 354 of the same ode.

O joy! that in our embers
Is something that doth live,
That nature yet remembers
What was so fugitive!
The thought of our past years in me doth breed
Perpetual benedictions: not indeed
For that which is most worthy to be blest;
Delight and liberty, the simple creed
Of childhood, whether busy or at rest,
With new-fledged hope still fluttering in his breast:—
Not for these I raise
The song of thanks and praise;
But for those obstinate questionings
Of sense and outward things,
Fallings from us, vanishings;
Blank misgivings of a creature
Moving about in worlds not realized,
High instincts, before which our mortal nature
Did tremble like a guilty thing surprised!
But for those first affections,
Those shadowy recollections,
Which, be they what they may,
Are yet the fountain light of all our day,
Are yet a master light of all our seeing;
Uphold us—cherish—and have power to make
Our noisy years seem moments in the being
Of the eternal silence; truths that wake
    To perish never:
Which neither listlessness, nor mad endeavor,
Nor man nor boy,

Nor all that is at enmity with joy,
Can utterly abolish or destroy!
Hence, in a season of calm weather,
Though inland far we be,
Our souls have sight of that immortal sea
Which brought us hither;
Can in a moment travel thither—
And see the children sport upon the shore,
And hear the mighty waters rolling evermore.

And since it would be unfair to conclude with an extract
which, though highly characteristic, must yet, from the
nature of the thoughts and the subject, be interesting,
or perhaps intelligible, to but a limited number of read-
ers; I will add from the poet's last published work a
passage equally Wordsworthian; of the beauty of which,
and of the imaginative power displayed therein, there can
be but one opinion, and one feeling. See "White Doe,"
page 5.

Fast the church-yard fills;—anon
Look again, and they all are gone;
The cluster round the porch, and the folk
Who sate in the shade of the prior's oak!
And scarcely have they disappeared
Ere the prelusive hymn is heard:—
With one consent the people rejoice,
Filling the church with a lofty voice!
They sing a service which they feel,
For 'tis the sun-rise now of zeal;
And faith and hope are in their prime
In great Eliza's golden time.

A moment ends the fervent din,
And all is hushed, without and within;
For though the priest, more tranquilly,
Recites the holy liturgy,
The only voice which you can hear
Is the river murmuring near.
When soft!—the dusky trees between,
And down the path through the open green,
Where is no living thing to be seen;
And through yon gateway, where is found,
Beneath the arch with ivy bound,
Free entrance to the church-yard ground;
And right across the verdant sod,
Towards the very house of God;
Comes gliding in with lovely gleam,

Comes gliding in serene and slow,
Soft and silent as a dream,
A solitary doe!
White she is as lily of June,
And beauteous as the silver moon
When out of sight the clouds are driven
And she is left alone in heaven;
Or like a ship some gentle day
In sunshine sailing far away,
A glittering ship, that hath the plain
Of ocean for her own domain.

   *   *   *   *   *   *

What harmonious pensive changes
Wait upon her as she ranges
Round and through this pile of state
Overthrown and desolate!
Now a step or two her way
Is through space of open day,
Where the enamoured sunny light
Brightens her that was so bright;
Now doth a delicate shadow fall,
Falls upon her like a breath,
From some lofty arch or wall,
As she passes underneath.

The following analogy will, I am apprehensive, appear
dim and fantastic, but in reading Bartram's *Travels* I
could not help transcribing[42] the following lines as a sort
of allegory, or connected simile and metaphor of Words-
worth's intellect and genius.—"The soil is a deep, rich,
dark mould, on a deep stratum of tenacious clay; and that
on a foundation of rocks, which often break through both
strata, lifting their back above the surface. The trees
which chiefly grow here are the gigantic black oak;
magnolia magniflora; fraxinus excelsior; platane; and a
few stately tulip trees." What Mr. Wordsworth *will* pro-
duce, it is not for me to prophesy: but I could pronounce
with the liveliest convictions what he is capable of pro-
ducing. It is the FIRST GENUINE PHILOSOPHIC
POEM. . . .[43]

[42] **transcribing** entry 926 of his notebooks (ed. Kathleen Coburn,
1957), March 26, 1801. See also William Bartram's *Travels*
(Facsimile Library, New York, 1940), pp. 55-56.
[43] **POEM** four pages of anticlimax are omitted here

BIBLIOGRAPHY

WORDSWORTH'S PREFACES

Preface to Lyrical Ballads, ed. W. J. B. Owen (Copenhagen, 1957). Anglistica, IX [Excellent critical edition].
Poetical Works, ed. Ernest de Selincourt (Oxford, 1944), Vol. II, pp. 383-462 [Variorum text of the Prefaces].
Literary Criticism, ed. N. C. Smith (London, 1905).

COLERIDGE'S *Biographia Literaria*

Pub. London, 1817; eds. H. N. and Sara Coleridge (London, 1847); John Shawcross (Oxford, 1907); George Sampson (Cambridge, 1920); George Watson (London, 1956).
Coleridge's Shakespearean Criticism, ed. T. M. Raysor (Cambridge, Mass., 1930). [Cf. I, 163-67; II, 64-99, with *Biog. Lit.*].

CRITICS OF WORDSWORTH AND COLERIDGE

ABRAMS, M. H., "Wordsworth and Coleridge on Diction and Figures," *English Institute Essays—1952* (New York, 1954).
———, *The Mirror and The Lamp* (New York, 1953).
BARSTOW, Marjorie L., *Wordsworth's Theory of Poetic Diction* (New Haven, 1917).
CRANE, R. S., "The Critical Monism of Cleanth Brooks," *Modern Philology,* May, 1948 (Rptd. in *Critics and Criticism,* ed. Crane, Chicago, 1952).
RICHARDS, I. A., *Coleridge on Imagination* (Cambridge, 1934).
WELLEK, René, *A History of Modern Criticism: 1750-1950* (Vols. I-II. New Haven, 1955).